Cosmic Ordering in 7 Easy Steps

Cosmic Ordering in 7 Easy Steps

How to Make Life Work for You

*

Carolyn Boyes

Collins

Collins
An imprint of HarperCollins Publishers
77–85 Fulham Palace Road, London w6 8jb

www.collins.co.uk

First published in 2006
Copyright © 2006 Carolyn Boyes

10 09 08 07 06

2

The author asserts her moral right to be
identified as the author of this work.

A catalogue record for this book is
available from the British Library.

isbn-10 0-00-724815-6
isbn-13 978-0-00-724815-5

Collins uses papers that are natural,
renewable and recyclable products made
from wood grown in sustainable forests.
The manufacturing processes conform
to the environmental regulations of the
country of origin.

Printed and bound in Great Britain
by Clays Ltd, St Ives plc

**Warning: Relaxation and self-hypnosis
exercises should not be attempted while
driving or operating machinery.**

Contents

The frog in the well

A frog lived deep down at the bottom of a well below a big blue sea. He had stones and broken bits of brick and tile to hop around every day and was very satisfied with his wonderful home.

One day a giant turtle swam past the opening of the well. He looked down the well and called out a greeting to the frog. The frog invited the turtle to come down into the well to see his wonderful home, but the turtle's body was so big only his head fit into the opening of the well.

'Tell me about the sea,' said the frog. 'Is it as big as my home?'

'Why,' replied the turtle, 'I can't even fit into your well. How can I possibly even compare the two – a small well and a vast ocean?'

The frog on hearing this couldn't believe it. 'How can your sea be in any way as wonderful as my well?'

TRADITIONAL CHINESE STORY

Introduction

'As ye think ye shall be.'

Proverb

What do you want to change in your life? How many unrealised hopes and dreams do you have? Perhaps in the past you have asked for what you wanted and been disappointed.

Perhaps you have had some success and want to have more?

Or maybe you just have a sense that something is missing and you want help to define it.

You probably already have some, or even many, ideas about what you would like to bring more of into your life. Maybe you want more of something in only one part of your life – more money or more time?

Perhaps you want something new – a relationship or a job?

How about what you want less of? Stress, unhappiness, fear or illness?

Your answer may well be, of course, 'Yes, but I don't have any choice.'

If so, perhaps like the frog in the well, you haven't noticed that there is an ocean of possibilities waiting for you out there. The universe is full of opportunities: you don't need to know how to *find* them, just how to *accept* them.

Imagine just for a moment that you really can have everything you want to have, be or do in your life today. How? Through cosmic ordering.

Cosmic ordering is very simple. If you ask for what you want and expect to receive it, the universe will give it to you. The good news is that this 'cosmic ordering' really does work.

So why don't you already have everything you want in your life right now? Well, like all simple things, they are only simple once you understand a few principles.

When you place an order with the universe, it is certain that the cosmic storehouse always has it in stock and will deliver it to you. However – and this is the big however – as I have learnt over years of experimentation and study, it will only work if you follow the magic formula.

As with everything that is simple, we can, and do, often make things more complicated than they need to be. So when you read on, you will discover ways to cut through the complications and create simplicity again.

Here are some of the ways you can use cosmic ordering to make your life better right now:

 You can stop attracting events, people and circumstances you don't want

 You can define your dreams and your life direction and purpose

 You can find the perfect relationship you have always wanted

You can create your ideal job and manifest money and possessions

 You can bring new people into your life as friends or business customers

 You can attract positive feelings on a daily basis

It is your choice. I will repeat it again. You really, really can and will create what you want. There are wonderful opportunities waiting for you right now.

You can lead a drab, dull life. You can feel trapped in the rat race. You can feel fear, anger, frustration, depression, irritation and other negative feelings...

Or you can soar and fly. You can create prosperity, you can feel happiness, excitement, fun and joy daily in your life.

How to read *Cosmic Ordering in 7 Easy Steps*

Cosmic Ordering in 7 Easy Steps is a practical, step-by-step guide and workbook that you can use to create what you want in your life through cosmic ordering.

Each technique and exercise in this book is there because it is the best way to empower you to achieve consistent results in your cosmic ordering. If you follow the formula to the letter, your results will be guaranteed.

When you read the book, make sure you read it from front to back. When you understand each step, read the magic formula starting on page 197 – you will then be ready to place your first order. You could go straight to that chapter, but it won't mean much to you unless you have worked through the workbook step by step.

Each time you place an order, make a note of what results you get. Your results are the only measure that matters. When you pay attention to your results, you will see how effectively you are ordering according to the magic formula and, if need be, which steps to pay most attention to.

Just by setting your intention to begin the process, your dreams are already starting to come true...

Don't be surprised if one comes true straight away.

Step 1:
Understand how the universe operates

'Some men go through a forest and see no firewood.'

ENGLISH PROVERB

Shopping in the cosmos

The way we shop has changed a great deal over the last few years. You no longer have to go tramping around a local high street from shop to shop to find what you are looking for; you can go to the internet, search for what you want and order it on screen. You place your order, a confirmation comes back and days or weeks later the item is delivered.

Between the placing of the order and the delivery to your doorstep a lot goes on. The order is received and processed, the item is checked out of the warehouse, dispatched and delivered. All of this is based on trust. You can't see it happening, but you are confident that behind the scenes the system is working efficiently on your behalf and, after a short interval, your order will be delivered. All you have to do is to go about your business in the normal way and accept delivery when the item arrives.

Of course, from time to time there may be a glitch in the system. Maybe the order didn't go through properly, or there is a delay and the item has to be reordered. Sometimes a similar item arrives but in a different colour to the one you ordered. What do you do then? You have a choice either to accept the item that has been dispatched, or to ask again for your original item. Most people expect to continue the process until they receive exactly what they asked for.

Nowadays, you can order just about everything on the internet – a book, a car, a job; you might even find your soul mate through an on-line date.

The cosmos or universe is like a vast and infinitely abundant on-line storehouse, but it is more than simply a consumer paradise – you can change your life by what you order. Yes, certainly, you can order material possessions to come your way, but you can also ask for happiness, prosperity, joy, fulfilment, enlightenment and understanding.

How does this amazing universal storehouse work?

It's a very simple system. Decide what you want, in any area of your life. Place your order and wait, knowing absolutely that you will receive it. You may have to wait in the meantime for what you want to appear in your life, but you know that all the while the cosmic system is making sure that what you want is being safely checked out of the storehouse and made ready for delivery.

The first step of the cosmic ordering process is to understand how the universe works.

Just as the internet operates according to rules and principles, even though it exists in the abstract world of cyberspace, so does the universe. You can only make a wish turn into reality if you order from the cosmos in a way that is as clear and logical as ordering from the internet.

A few things about the way life is

Have you been told something like this? Here are a few of the things you may have been told at least once in your life that aren't particularly helpful:

- Life is tough
- Life isn't a game
- You have to suffer to get anywhere in life

- You will have to work hard to get what you want
- Miracles don't happen in real life
- There's only so much to go around
- Life isn't supposed to be fun
- You can't have everything you want in life
- If you aren't clever enough you won't succeed
- If you aren't beautiful enough you won't succeed
- Some people get all the luck
- Lucky people are born not made
- Dreams are just a fantasy
- This is real life...

Did you believe whoever told you that you were limited in the life you could have?

Even though children generally expect to be given what they ask for, very few adults expect life to fulfil their dreams in the same way. In fact, many of us learn the opposite – we think we have to struggle, we think we have to use willpower to achieve anything and everything in life.

Many people believe that the more effort you put into something the more likely you are to get a result. But is that really true? Does struggle and hard work really guarantee a result? If it did, wouldn't the hardest-working person always be the most successful? We know that is not always true. The most talented person isn't necessarily the person who is happiest or has the best career. The most intelligent boy at school isn't the one who grows up to make the most money. The prettiest girl isn't the one who wins the heart of the most handsome man in the room.

So why do some people achieve their dreams and others don't?

People whose dreams come true are those who pursue their dreams in a way that is in tune with the universe. The truth is, you don't have to struggle; you don't have to work hard; you don't have to use willpower to make your dreams come true. You can live your life as happily as in a fairy tale – the one where the prince always wins his bride, the ugly duckling becomes a swan, and Cinderella turns into a princess.

But life isn't really like that, is it? If you aren't getting what you want from life, no matter what that is – happiness, success, possessions or love – stick to your old beliefs about the universe and nothing will change.

The secret is that the universe, just as in a fairy tale, really can provide you with anything your *heart* desires (not what your *head* desires). If you open your mind up to new possibilities, new possibilities will open their opportunities up to you.

The secrets of the universe

The operating principles of the universe aren't the invention of some New Age guru. They have been known to every ancient tradition on the planet for thousands of years. But in the past they were regarded as a great secret, only to be passed on to those initiates who were mature enough to be able to use their knowledge wisely. In some traditions you couldn't learn this knowledge until you were at least 40 years old.

But these secrets are in reality available to anyone who is open to the knowledge. In fact, nowadays the ideas that were once seen as so special do not seem obscure, thanks to the huge leaps in scientific understanding that have been made over the last one hundred years or so. After all, many of the things we take for granted now would once have been regarded by our ancestors as impossible or in the realms of magic.

The 1st secret: The universe is infinite

Scientists have established that the universe is vast. It is composed of particles so small that they can be measured only by the most advanced technology.

You and I can see the world we live in through our senses – we see objects with our eyes, we can feel objects by touching them, we can smell and taste them. But the universe is much bigger than the physical universe you can see, hear, taste, smell and feel. Just as you can't see the systems inside your body that ensure you keep breathing, or that make your limbs move, or run your digestive system, much of the universe is outside your sensory experience. According to most ancient philosophies, there is a vast invisible universe that exists alongside the world you are aware of. It is so vast, in fact, that it is infinite – without beginning and end.

The 2nd secret: Everything in the universe has its own vibration

The universe is not static. Everything in the universe is composed of energy: atoms, molecules and subatomic particles. All of these vibrate at particular frequencies. Science has shown that whether it is our physical selves or the objects in our environment, everything has its own vibration. Why this is important you will see below in the Law of Attraction (p.21).

The 3rd secret: We live in a mental world

The universe is actually a vast intelligence whose purpose is to constantly translate thoughts and ideas into what we call reality. Many religions or philosophies have set out the secret of universal intelligence – that mind is always dominant over matter, even in the first ever creation process.

The word 'mind' is often used to describe this intelligence, but this can be misleading, because it causes many people to believe that it is enough to think consciously about what they want, while, in fact, the process is more subtle than that, as you will see in *Step 4: Take charge of your thoughts*.

> *'In the beginning God created the heaven and the*
> *earth. And the earth was without form, and void;*
> *and darkness was upon the face of the deep. And the*
> *Spirit of God moved upon the face of the waters.'*

> Genesis 1:1–2

'God' referred to in the Christian tradition can also be referred to as the cosmic or universal intelligence. The universe is created and constantly recreated by this intelligence. In fact, this intelligence exists within every atom of the universe and every cell of our body. Without this intelligence, as it says in Genesis, there is simply a void. The form or physical matter of the world is only created because of the power of the universal mind. You don't have to believe in God or a particular religion for this to work. You just have to allow for the possibility that it will – and be pleasantly surprised when it does.

How does the process of creating something from nothing work?

- Before anything exists there is nothing – only a void in which no shape or form exists
- A thought or idea of something penetrates the void
- As soon as this happens, the idea can be made manifest – into a real living object, person, or event in our physical world

Because thought guides the universe, energy is directed to whatever the mind focuses on and becomes manifest as a reality.

Everything that currently exists in the world first existed in the cosmic mind as an idea *before* it existed in physical form – you, the work you do, the place you live, the money you earn, the person and people you love, the plants, the trees, the whole country.

The 4th secret: The Great Secret – *you* are the co-creator

'But I didn't create the plants and the trees and the world around me,' you may say.

It is true: you *didn't* create them; the cosmic intelligence did. But you *do* have the power to create an entirely different life for yourself. You can create events, experiences, physical possessions or relationships.

In your own life you are co-creator with the cosmos – this is the great secret that is known to all magical traditions. Even though you may not realise it, you are constantly creating your future, together with the universe.

The ancient Hawaiians had a good explanation for how this process takes place. They believed that each person had three selves – a conscious mind, an unconscious mind, and a higher self. What you think, consciously and unconsciously, is instantly transmitted to your higher self. The higher self creates your future out of all your thoughts and desires whether you are conscious of them or not. Moreover, each higher self is able to link to the higher selves of all other people in the world and to the mind of the universe, and together this shared or group mind links to the cosmic intelligence and constantly creates the common future of all of us.

What is certain is that if you send a thought into the cosmos, the cosmos will answer your order. A cosmic order is simply a way of making sure that the thoughts you send are intentional and create the future you desire, rather than an accidental future caused by the jumble of your daily thoughts.

The 5th secret: The universe is infinitely abundant

As you become more and more proficient in the ordering process and more and more in tune with the cosmic mind, you will be able to use ideas more precisely and create precisely the kind of life you dream of having, rather than being at the whim of fate.

There is nothing that is withheld from you. The universal storehouse never runs out of anything because the mind can never run out of ideas.

Anything and *everything* can be created through the mind of the invisible universe and then materialised or manifested within the visible world.

The 6th secret: The universe is impartial

The universe treats all of us equally. You have as much right as anyone else to ask the universe for anything you want. It creates everything without favouritism: it has no self-interest.

The 7th secret: Time and space only exist in the physical part of the universe

In the non-physical part of the universe – the part that cannot be sensed through sight, hearing, feeling, taste or smell – there is no time and space. Time and space are concepts of the material world. In the rest of the universe it is always *Now*. The Future, Past and Present are all the same.

When you bypass the rules of time and space and link up to the vast invisible universe, you too can for a moment be outside time. The cosmic ordering process uses this knowledge. You have all the power you need right now. You can link to the resources of your past, you can recreate a memory, or put a future memory into your future (as you will see in *Step 6: Place your order*).

The moment you place a cosmic order, the universe registers it immediately and gets ready to deliver it to you.

Five truths about you and the universe

- This is a 'thought' universe and so the world is what you think it is
- All power comes from within, so you have the power to create a different life for yourself
- You are unlimited. The universe is unlimited and so everything is possible

- Energy flows to wherever you focus and your attention goes
- The moment of power is always now

The two Universal Laws

The Universal Laws are the principles that bind the universe together. They have arisen from a variety of ancient traditions and constitute widely recognised New Age theories. You can't transgress a Law: they can't be disobeyed. You can't see them, but the evidence for their existence is in the results you get in your life. Like gravity, they exist as an abstract concept outside our immediate awareness, but have a very real and constant effect on our lives.

The Universal Laws operate consistently all the time and cannot be bent.

The Law of Attraction

The Law of Attraction is working in your life right now. The circumstances, job, relationships and friends you have, or don't have, are all what you have attracted according to the energy and vibration you are transmitting.

You are like a magnet. You will attract what you focus on and think about, whether or not it is something you consciously want. The Law of Attraction is the most powerful force underlying the universe. You can't overcome it.

As we have seen, everything in the universe vibrates and is moving. According to the Law of Attraction, when something vibrates at a particular frequency, it attracts and resonates with other things vibrating at the same frequency.

Thoughts as well as objects have their own vibration. You attract particular events towards you, according to the frequency of the vibration of your thoughts.

Whatever you give your attention to, you will attract. This doesn't have to be conscious attention. The conscious mind is only a tiny part of our mind. The greater part of it is unconscious, so whatever is fed into your unconscious you attract into your reality. If you have thoughts that attack or are in conflict with each other, you will attract a jumble of experiences – what most of us call 'reality' or 'normality'.

The cosmic ordering process enables you to work with the Law of Attraction and become a deliberate thinker and creator of what you want to attract into your life. As you follow the process, you will become much more aware of the link between your thoughts and the experiences you attract to you. You will learn more about this in *Step 4: Take charge of your thoughts.*

The Law of Cause and Effect, or Consequences

This law is often referred to as Karma – it gives us a sense of responsibility alongside our power as co-creators of our own destinies.

- What we sow, we subsequently reap
- What comes around goes around
- What you put out you will get back
- For every action there is an equal and opposite reaction

You sow with your thoughts, words and deeds, and reap the effect in your own reality. Your will is always and will be done. As Deepak Chopra once said, 'There is a perfect accounting system in the universe.' If you run up a debt on one side of your balance sheet, it will be paid off on the other side. If you run up a credit, it will likewise be balanced out.

Part of the cosmic ordering process is taking responsibility for what reality you want to create and being clear why you think that it will be beneficial for your life.

The more you practise the process and see the results that you get, the wiser you will become in what you ask for. Many people find that because of this they move away from placing cosmic orders relating to possessions, and ask for greater and wiser things in their life that will bring them experiences out of which they will learn and grow in understanding.

Later in the book, you will be shown how to keep an order delivery diary – to build your personal record of evidence for what results have been caused by you. Keeping this diary will act as a record of the consequences of the orders you place.

> *When you are grateful in advance for what you are about to receive, you can achieve your dreams successfully, and quickly!*

Tip **Gratitude**

- The universe responds to gratitude. When you become grateful for all the experiences you have attracted into your life, whether you have classified them as negative or positive in the past, the universe rewards you. Being grateful ensures that we learn and understand from our experiences in the material world.

- The universe sends us the events and situations we need to grow, learn and develop as human beings. Each time you recognise and acknowledge, through your expression of gratitude, the gifts that a particular experience has given you, the universe recognises that you are ready to move on and sends you a new experience.

- Say thank you as often as possible for all you have gone through, and really notice what benefits you have got from each experience life has thrown your way. Doing this teaches you to embrace and cherish what life has to offer you, which is in effect what you have yourself created.

- When you are grateful for what you have attracted, you automatically attract more good things into your life. By holding this spirit of gratitude, you can now deliberately ask the universe from your heart to bring specific new experiences into your life. Because the old events now hold no energy or vibration other than a positive one, the universe is open to co-create positive events in your future with you. You create these events by thanking the universe in advance for what it is about to give you.

Summary Step 1

- Understand and work with the secrets and laws of the universe and you will see enormous changes happening in your life.
- Of course, you can't not work with the universe. But from now on, you can deliberately choose your thoughts and actions in full awareness of what you are doing.
- Pay attention to the Laws of Attraction and Cause and Effect.
- Express your gratitude to the universe.

Step 2:

Decide what you want

'The thoughts that come so often unsought, and... as it were, drop into the mind, are commonly the most valuable of any we have. And therefore should be secured, because they seldom return again.'

JOHN LOCKE

What do you want?

What were you going to be when you grew up? Have your dreams been fulfilled?

When you were a child, looking into the future, did you imagine your present life as it is now?

When we are children we take imagination for granted. You dream that you will be rich, successful or famous. Maybe you will travel the world. Perhaps you will own a big house or fast car. Perhaps you will ride a camel across the desert or fly a plane around the world.

What would it be like if you could make those dreams come true now? True, some of your dreams may have changed. Or maybe many of them are as they have always been?

How would it be if you could believe that even *one* of your dreams could turn into reality?

Maybe you know exactly what you want, maybe you have only a slight inkling, or maybe no ideas at all. Or, perhaps you even need to be convinced that it is okay to dream at all?

Whichever way, you probably want something to change in *at least* some part of your life. In this step, you will start the process of laying the foundations for changing your life by discovering and rediscovering your dreams.

Your life right now

'For all sad words of tongue and pen,
The saddest are these: "It might have been".'

JOHN GREENLEAF WHITTIER

How satisfied are you?

Take a look at your life as it is right now.

Your life is as it is right now because you have created it.

'That's not fair,' you might reply. 'I haven't created my life to be like this. Of course I would like to have more money, a better relationship, a happier social life, children, a new job, but I "have to" do what I do and this is why I want and need all these things.'

It may surprise you to discover that you have always had all the means inside you to create anything in your life you want to – to create a unique expression of who you are.

The reasons we have for all the things we 'have to' or 'should' or 'must' do are illusions. Your present is your present. Your past is your past. Your future can be entirely different. The power to make a new future is not dependent on your circumstances; it is dependent only on your mind.

You can have what you want in the future, no matter what is happening in your life right now and what has happened in the past.

Anna's story:
The case of the right apartment

I was living in a big house on the outskirts of London. My children had left home and I thought that it was time to swap all the space I no longer needed for a bijou apartment in the centre of the city.

I knew exactly what I was looking for: I visualised a flat with French windows and a large sitting room, a balcony and a roof terrace. Everybody kept saying, 'It's not possible. There isn't the availability. You can't get all those things together.' But I kept imagining myself in a flat just like that.

After looking for a while, I found a flat that wasn't exactly like the one I imagined, but I went for it anyway. However, after I put in the offer, the seller took it off the market. I then went on holiday, a bit fed up with the process. Going on holiday gave me the chance to recollect my thoughts and think again about what I really wanted.

While I was away, my estate agent phoned me to tell me that he had three more apartments for me to see. I came back to London and he telephoned me again, but when I heard the details I wasn't keen to see them as they were too expensive.

Eventually, when he realised that I wasn't interested, he told me about another apartment. He hadn't bothered to tell me about it originally because he wouldn't have got the same commission on it.

I went to see it, and, of course, it was my dream flat. It needed lots of work doing to it – the bathroom would need changing around totally, the pipes replacing, the floor and

the paintwork would all take money to fix – but it had the
French windows and the large sitting room, the balcony
and a roof terrace at the back, and it was right in the
centre of London.

What's more, even though it's a busy part of town,
now I have moved in, I always get a parking space. Even
when it seems impossible, someone always clears out of a
space just when I am looking for one!

Deciding what you want

This series of exercises will help you develop your thinking
about what you want in your life in preparation for the next
step, where you will learn how to change your dreams into
more specific cosmic orders.

You don't have to do all the exercises. Choose the ones
that appeal to you most. They are designed to stimulate your
imagination so that you can be absolutely clear about what you
really want – something that is totally personal and right
for you.

What is my life like now?

One way to think about what you want is to
consider how satisfied you are currently in the various
areas of your life. You can divide your life up in different ways, of course, but here is a starting point for your
thinking: *How much joy, happiness, satisfaction and*
fulfilment do you have currently in each area?

How many marks out of ten would you currently give each area? Write your current score on the chart below.

Area of life   **Level of current satisfaction**

(Give this area a mark out of ten)

Social   _____/10

Romantic relationship   _____/10

Health and fitness   _____/10

Money   _____/10

Personal development   _____/10

Family   _____/10

Career   _____/10

Spiritual growth   _____/10

✎ Raising my satisfaction to ten out of ten

Use this chart as a starting point for your thinking about what you want in your life. Notice where you would most like to see change and a higher level of satisfaction.

- Select an area from the chart opposite that you have given a low mark to.
- Ask yourself: 'For this area what would I have to create to bring my score up to ten out of ten for satisfaction, joy and fulfilment?'
- In the section below, write some initial thoughts about this area.

Area of life	Initial thoughts: what would raise my satisfaction levels to ten out of ten?
Example *Social life: currently not active enough for me so rated 5/10.*	*Going out once or twice a week in the evening. Speaking on a daily basis to at least one friend. Going dancing twice a month. Learning a new skill over the next year.*

If you like, you can now repeat this process for any other areas of your life to which you gave a low score.

✒️ What do I believe is in my future now?

What you want to be in your future is not necessarily what you believe to be in your future now. So that you can see the gap between what you want and your current reality, take a look into the future: What do you believe your future will be like from the vantage point you have right now?

Ask yourself:

- *What do I want to change about my future?*
- *What would make my life far more exciting?*
- *What would make me happier?*
- *What would make my life more adventurous?*
- *What would make my life more fun?*
- *What would make me feel fulfilled?*
- *What would make me feel joyous?*

Write down any immediate thoughts that you have.

....

....

....

....

....

What will life be like when I am:

30

Example: *I see myself as single, getting promoted in my career, living where I live currently. I want to get married, but when I look into my future I can't see this yet.*

40

Example: *I see myself living somewhere different – I have a sense of countryside with animals around. I feel I am travelling a lot and having some adventures.*

50

Example: *I have a feeling that I am with a partner in a relationship, but I can't see children even though I want them.*

60

Example: *I have a picture of me with a family, but I am not sure they are blood relatives – maybe stepchildren?*

....

....

....

70

Example: *I have a feeling that I have quite a few friends here, but I realise I'm concerned about money and feeling old – although I always hoped to be rich at 70. Maybe it is because my parents always worried about being poor when they were older?*

....

....

....

80

Example: *I have a feeling of being myself and doing something adventurous.*

....

....

....

90

Example: *I realise I have no vision of my life currently past 80 because my parents died before this age. It means I want to change this so I have a future after 90.*

....

....

....

What do you love doing?

Here's an exercise to get you thinking about what works for you at present and what you might want to keep in any future you create.

Think back to a time in your past when you did something that felt 100 per cent right.

What was it about the experience that felt right?

What feeling did it give you?

Who was there with you at the time?

What was present in the experience that is not normally present?

What was absent from the experience that is normally present?

What changes can you make in your life to reflect what you have learnt from what you have written?

Your childhood dreams

The next exercise makes sure that you take account of any unfulfilled dreams you still have.

What did you love doing when you were a child?

....

....

....

....

What dreams did you have when you were young?

....

....

What dreams do you still want to be fulfilled?

....

....

Write down any additional thoughts that you have.

....

....

....

....

✏️ If I started over…

Consider, for a moment, if you were to start your life again right now, what would you want?

What's important to you?

_____

_____

What do you have already in your life that you would want to keep?

_____

_____

What people would you keep in your life?

_____

_____

If you had total choice in how you spent your time, where would you focus your attention?

_____

_____

_____

If you were to travel ten years into the future and look back at the present, what would really be important?

_____

_____

_____

If you were to travel to the end of your life and look back, what would you want to have spent your time doing more of?

_____

_____

If you were to travel to the end of your life and look back, who would you have wanted to spend your time with?

_____

_____

Tip What do you want?

- Whatever you ask the cosmos for, there's no point in asking for something you feel you 'have to', or 'should', or 'must' have.

- There's no point in placing lots of orders that are what someone else wants rather than what you want. Why not ask for something you _really_ want to have, that you feel _inspired_ to have, that you want _from your heart_ not your head?

Being, doing and having

Here's another way to stimulate your thinking about what you may want. All wants can be put under three categories:

- What you want to *be*
- What you want to *do*
- What you want to *have*

The universe can deliver an order in any of these categories. When you think about what you want, think under all three headings. On the worksheet below, jot down any initial thoughts about what you would like to *be*, *do* or *have* in your life.

What do I want to be?

_____

_____

What do I want to do?

_____

_____

What do I want to have?

_____

_____

_____

_____

Creating inspiration

Seeking inspiration

How do you begin if you have written down some good ideas but are still lacking real inspiration about what to ask for?

There are times in life when you get a feeling inside yourself that you want something different to happen. It is like a distant radio signal that you can't quite tune into. But it gets stronger and stronger until the day comes when you feel an irresistible urge to do something about it. Yet how can you act if you still don't know what to do, or what you want, but you just know that it is something that you don't yet have in your life?

Inspiration is a communication from the universe, it can't be forced into existence logically. It is from the Latin word *inspirare*, literally meaning to 'breathe into', or indicating that God has breathed upon the one inspired, so you are taking in 'spirit'. This is why inspiration can feel as if it's just dropped into your mind from nowhere. Because your brain loves pictures and images much more than words, you can inspire ideas by feeding your mind with pictures.

The following exercises will create pictures in your mind and stimulate your unconscious so that inspiration just pops into your head when you are least expecting it.

Your dream picture

If you only have a few ideas about what you may want in your life, a dream picture is a highly effective way of beginning to stimulate your imagination.

Collect a pile of magazines, as many as you can find. Give yourself some space. Sit down with a pair of scissors and start cutting out any pictures of objects, people, situations and places that inspire you. You will find that you become surprisingly discriminating as you do this, rejecting some outright.

 Next, either take a piece of flip-chart paper and glue the pictures on in a collage, or pin them onto a kitchen-style notice board. The important things are that you are entirely intuitive about where you place each picture and that you can put your finished collage somewhere in your home where you can look at it regularly.

 The best place to position your dream picture is somewhere you pass by several times a day, so that you catch sight of your inspirational pictures regularly. This way, they will feed your imagination with positive images of your future. If you are using a notice board, you can add other items as well as magazine pictures – maybe photographs of you in happy situations, postcards, or objects that remind you of things you want in your life.

Your box of dreams

An alternative to a dream picture is to have a box specifically in which to keep bits and pieces that capture your imagination in some way. If this works well for you, use this method. I prefer the dream picture, because you are likely to see it frequently in passing, whereas you may not open your box as often. The more you see pictures or items that feed your imagination, the more your imagination will be fired up.

Remember: What is important to you?

People who do what they want are doing so for no other reason than because it matters to them. This applies whether they are in business, a writer, an artist or a refuse collector.

Suppose you get to a certain point in your life, yet you still aren't happy. Perhaps you have millions in the bank. Maybe you have a great family, a big house, all the trappings. If all this still leaves you feeling empty, then it's because you don't have a life that really matters to you.

What is important to you in all the different contexts of your life is unique to you. Only you have the ability, the gift (and the responsibility) to decide what should be important to you.

However, one advantage of using a box is that you can put actual objects into it, and the sensory experience of taking the objects out and physically touching them can be a very positive way of stimulating your imagination.

Where have you got to in your thinking about what you want?

At this stage of your thinking, you may have some very specific ideas about what you want to create in your life. If you don't yet, that's fine, you can think in broad terms at the moment. For example, if you know that you want a new career but don't know what career that might be, picture yourself in a place of work that is happy and harmonious, where you feel fulfilled and are learning and progressing.

Or, suppose you would like to be in a relationship, then imagine being with someone who you are happy with, who you have fun with and love, and who loves you.

Perhaps you would like more money. Visualise a table in front of you piled high with banknotes and gold and precious gems. Imagine that you can spend as much as you want and yet the table will never be empty of cash.

Creating broad images will get your imagination kickstarted and you will automatically find that you start to see more images of what you want in your life. Moreover, as soon as you start the process, the universe will throw events and people into your path to show you what it is possible for you to have within the vision you have outlined.

✏️ My dream pie

Make sure that you complete this exercise before continuing to the next step.

Now, use all the exercises you have completed so far and bake your ideas into a dream pie.

- Look back at everything you have written down so far about your dreams.
- Look back at *What is my life like now* on page 31 to remind yourself of the areas of your life in which you are least satisfied.

- Remember to make the distinction between what really matters to you and the things dictated by your current circumstances.
- Once you've identified something as being of value to you, imagine living life both with it and without it. If managing without it is not such a big deal then maybe it's not something that's of prime importance to you.
- Write down under the title of each life area what you would have to do to go from 10 per cent to 100 per cent satisfaction in your life.
- If you would prefer different titles for your life areas, write them in the extra boxes.

Tip **The importance of balance**

When you think about what you want, it is important to think about all the different areas of your life. If you simply place orders in one part of your life, the rest of your life may become out of balance. This can happen unintentionally. How many people can you think of who spend so much time thinking about their careers that they get exactly the success they crave, only to sacrifice a marriage or their health in the process? Or they swing the other way entirely, spending a lot of time building a good social and family life, but lose out on financial stability.

Area of life	Dreams

Social

Romantic relationship

Health and fitness

Money

Personal development

Family

Career

Spiritual growth

Summary Step 2

- First decide what you want.
- Look to your past dreams for inspiration.
- Collect pictures and objects to stimulate your imagination and create inspiration.
- Think about what you want.
- Make sure you think about what you want in all parts of your life.

Step 3:

Turn your wants into specific orders

'This above all – to thine own self be true;
And it must follow, as the night the day,
Thou canst not then be false to any man.'

SHAKESPEARE, *HAMLET*, I.III

You can choose your own destinations in life

Imagine that you wanted to go to South America on holiday. You'd probably start by buying a ticket. But where exactly would you buy a ticket to?

Would you step onto the aeroplane without being specific about your destination? Would you be equally happy to end up in Chile or Argentina?

Perhaps, when you go to the travel agent, you make a decision that where you really want to go to was Peru, but you don't specify where in Peru. Would it matter to you if you end up in the capital city or the countryside?

Sometimes it can be quite an adventure to see where you end up in life when you don't have a clear destination. The trouble is, you can end up with a few misadventures on the journey as well. And you may not like the destination you finally reach.

If you want to be certain you will enjoy yourself, it is better to be specific about where you want to go.

Yet in life, how many people happily drift along like a passenger without a destination, going wherever the plane chooses to fly, or perhaps like a rudderless boat adrift on the ocean, just floating with the tide, knowing only some general direction in which they are travelling?

The difference between wanting and ordering

In Step 3 you can start to apply the process of turning all the wants and dreams you have written down in Step 2 into individual cosmic orders. You do this by adding *focus* and *commitment* to your wants.

A want is just a longing or a desire without energy. 'I will' means that whatever happens, you won't stop until you get your desire. A wish is passive, a cosmic order is active: harnessing the power of the universe to fulfil your desire.

You may want to go to South America on holiday, but until you go and buy a ticket you are not going to get there. You may want to buy a car, but unless you make a decision to buy one, you are not committed, and you could change your mind and spend your money on your home or a holiday instead.

A cosmic order is a decision that you will have, be or do something new in your life; you will change in some way, you will have a result in your life that you haven't had before.

Each time you take a want and make it a cosmic order you are giving a clear instruction to the universe to deliver to you what you want, in the same way as an airline ticket has a clear instruction written down on it about where you want the pilot to fly you. You may not know all the details of the route he is going to take, but your ticket instructs him to take you to exactly the destination you want.

*The process of turning your wants into cosmic
orders is a five-part process.*

1: Be specific about what you want

As soon as you start to think about and write down your
dreams, you have already begun to become a deliberate creator
of your future. To make sure that you get more of what you
really want, think as specifically as possible about each dream
you have written down.

Why is this important? Because you really will get exactly
what you ask for. Remember the story of King Midas, the man
with the golden touch.

The story of King Midas
*King Midas was a king who loved gold. He already had a
storehouse full of gold, but he never spent any of it. He
lived just to take it out and count it and touch it, and loved
knowing he owned it.*

*One day he found a satyr lost in his garden – a half-
man, half-goat creature called Silenius, the teacher of the
god Dionysus. King Midas took Silenius back to his
student and Dionysus was so grateful to Midas for looking
after his friend that he granted him a wish. Midas
immediately knew what he wanted – more gold!*

*'I wish that I could turn everything I touch into gold,'
he said. Dionysus asked him, 'Are you certain you really
want this wish?' Midas was adamant. He returned to the*

palace happily turning over in his mind a picture of all the piles of gold he was going to own.

On his way back he walked through the palace gardens. He made his way underneath a beautiful arch of roses. One was trailing down and he reached towards it to pull it out of the way. The flower broke off – a rose once red but now turned to solid gold.

Excitedly, Midas touched another rose, then an apple from a nearby tree, then a pear. All were turned to gold. He put them in his pockets and as soon as he touched the cloth, that too turned to gold.

Midas walked into the palace laden down with all manner of beautiful golden fruit and plants. He sat down at the head of the great table where all his family and the courtiers were awaiting him. Midas couldn't wait to show off his gift to all his subjects. He reached for his wine goblet to take a sip, knowing that he would astound his guests by turning it to gold. Sure enough, as he touched it the goblet became solid gold. But as his lips touched the warm wine within, that too became hot liquid gold, scalding his lips. He felt for the food on the plate in front of him. The meat and the bread beneath his fingers turned to cold metal. He cried out with a start. His little daughter heard his cry and ran towards him calling, 'Daddy, are you hurt?' Midas reached for her, but as he touched her, with horror he saw her turn to solid gold – a statue frozen where a living child had stood.

Midas despaired and went to Dionysus to beg him to remove his accursed gift. Luckily, Dionysus took pity on him. He told Midas to cleanse himself in the nearby *stream. The water ran with gold as Midas washed himself and when he emerged the gift of gold was gone. When he returned to the palace, his daughter was once more a flesh and blood. Midas threw open the doors to the gold vaults and gave away or spent most of the gold. He resolved never again to be so miserly.*

To make your dreams specific, glance over your dream pie from pages 46-9. Look at each dream in turn. Think for a moment:

'What details can I add to this dream to make it as specific as possible?'

Later in this chapter you will learn the process by which you can change each of your wants into a specific order.

2: Add a delivery date

'When do I want this?' Part of being specific and sufficiently detailed is to think whether or not you want to have a specific date by which your order is to be delivered. The universe can oblige you quite easily because it can access the future as easily as the past and present: there is no concept of time in the part of the universe where your order is made ready for delivery.

You always have two choices with any cosmic order:

- You can simply ask for your order and not worry about when it will be delivered. The universe is perfectly happy to fill in those details for you as soon as you have visualised the order as if it is now present in your life.

- Or, you can also ask the universe very specifically for an order to be delivered on an exact date. A cosmic order can be as exact as you like. If you want to have a new career by 8 September this year, you can have one just as long as you follow all the steps laid out in this workbook. In fact, as you will see in the final part of this book, you can ask for a number of orders, one after another for the next six months, year or ten years and the universe can deliver each one of them exactly on time and exactly to your specifications. However, if, when the time comes around, you are not ready, you can block this process (see page 46).

When the universe knows best

Always allow for the possibility that the universe knows better than you about the best timing because it may have something even better to offer you. The universe's part in the co-creation process is to look after your highest good – and that may not be obvious to you at the time. The universe operates through love and so is not judgemental, but is loving.

When the universe holds back an order, you can think of it as your guardian angel or Higher Self looking after your best interests because they can see circumstances around the corner that you may not be aware of. Sometimes the universe helps us to go through a number of experiences first so that we can grow into our orders. With each experience, your ability to make a more specific and positive picture of what you really want grows.

Take this scenario: *you live in a small community in the Deep South of America and work in marketing as a full-time employee in a small workplace.*

What you really want and dream about is to change your life completely. You want to work as a self-employed seminar presenter travelling around Europe, Asia and the Middle East.

You can fill in some of the details of your dream because you have a great imagination and you have seen television pictures of some of the places where you want to travel.

But you want all this to happen within a year. Is it possible? Yes, absolutely. But *only* if the pictures in your mind have enough belief, desire and feeling attached to them.

Attach positive feeling to your picture

You may really want this dream in this time frame, and desire is important. But you also have to be able to *feel* the dream as if it is real (you will learn more about how to do this in *Step 6: Place your order*).

To every thought, a feeling is attached. The amount of feeling you put into your cosmic order governs how successfully it will be delivered. Just thinking with your head about what you want isn't enough.

Your dream needs to be as real to you in your imagination as anything you have experienced in the past. The more similar experiences you have had in the past, the more real your pictures will be. For example, if you have actually been to Europe, you will know what it feels like to be there. You may not have worked there already, but your pictures will probably appear more real to you than if you have simply used the television as inspiration.

When you are waiting for an order, the universe might not fulfil it in exactly the way you envisaged. Look closely at what has been sent and see if you have been given something even more helpful instead. The universe will always be helping you on your journey to growth and self-development.

For example, the progress of our employee moving from the Deep South to his new job around the world might go something like this:

The path to order

He is offered a job as a self-employed trainer if he moves to another town in America. It isn't the type of training he dreamt of, but at least it is training. (This allows him to get the feeling of being self-employed and to see other places in real life.)

He does this job for a year and is then offered the opportunity to start working for several companies. One of them has an office in Dubai. He travels there twice in the first few months. (He has now had the experience of working in another country outside America.)

He contacts a PR company in Dubai, which also has offices in London and Hong Kong. Can they market him as a trainer on the basis of his experience to date? They set up a seminar for him in Dubai. (Now the universe has thrown him an opportunity to start growing into a new role.)

He is very successful in Dubai and after six months he asks the PR company to start marketing him through their two other offices.

After 18 months of travel, he has a list of very satisfied clients. (He now knows what it feels like to be successful in his chosen field and has a much clearer picture of his end dream.)

He begins to branch out and within another year has developed a series of presentations much more in line with his own philosophy.

One day a businessman approaches him out of the blue. He says that he is so inspired by our dreamer's method of presentation, he would like to put up the money to market him as a seminar presenter around the world – in all the places our man originally dreamt of all those years ago. He now has his dream.

Tip Dream big

If you are asking for something significant that could change your life, make your order bigger, with a delivery date further away than you would ask for with a small order. The universe finds it easy to deliver big orders if they are far enough in the future because it can present you with a series of experiences that will allow you to grow into your dreams.

Give yourself time

So remember both to stretch your thinking and certainly write down your real, huge dreams and turn them into orders. At the same time, give the universe time to deliver your order to you.

Thinking back to the metaphor of flying, if you wanted to travel from Paris to London you wouldn't need to allow much time because the distance is relatively small. However, if you wanted to fly from England to Australia, you would need to allow a lot more time. During the flight you could sit back and relax while the pilot followed his route to get you there. It wouldn't matter if you had to make a stopover en route, you would still end up in Australia.

In fact, on long journeys like this, the pilot has to go off-course occasionally just to get the best flying conditions for the aeroplane, but he always makes adjustments to the route so that the plane can land on time.

3: Write your cosmic order down

Always write down your cosmic order. By writing it down rather than just thinking inside your head, you set out your intention much more strongly to the universe. Many people find that the process of writing something causes them to evaluate their feelings towards it in quite a different way than by simply turning it over inside their heads. It not only allows you to return and look with a fresh eye from time to time at what you have written, but the act of simply putting something on paper also builds an unconscious commitment to it.

✎ Write it down using the present tense

When you write down an order, always write it down in the present tense and make it personal. For example, 'I now have. I now am.'

The universe hears this as an instruction to deliver your order as soon as possible. It wants to make this true – you *do* already have your order. It is now waiting in the storehouse for you – ready for delivery.

Practise turning your wants into orders. Take three of your wants/dreams from your dream pie in Step 2 on pages 48–49 and turn them into cosmic orders. Be specific and commit now to having what you want.

Name of dream	Specifics written in the present tense and personal to you
Example	
I want a new car	It is July 2007. I now have a new Mercedes. It is silver coloured with this year's registration.

Name of dream 1	Specifics

Name of dream 2   Specifics

• •

Name of dream 3   Specifics

4: When you know what you don't want, but you don't know what you do want

Sometimes you may be able to be very specific, but only about what you want to move away from, rather than what you want to move towards.

For example, you might say, 'I don't want to be poor. I don't want another relationship like that one. I don't want this job any more.'

So what happens if you place an order for something you don't want?

You will get what you ask for, so take care to ask for what you really want.

As we've seen, the universe functions according to the Law of Attraction (see page 21). You attract exactly what you ask for and the universe does not process negatives.

So if you think, 'I don't want a relationship like the last one', the universe doesn't take account of the word 'don't' in the sentence and hears instead 'a relationship like the last one'.

For example, don't think of a pink elephant standing next to a tree. No, really. Don't think of a pink elephant standing next to a tree. What are you thinking of?

Now – *do* think of a blue elephant holding a stick in his trunk. It is always more effective to focus on what you do want than what you don't want.

Check how you have written down your dreams so far. If any of them are written in negatively phrased language, think about how you can write down what you would like instead.

Turning 'don't wants' into positive specific wants.

If you have a dream from Step 2 that you have written in negatively phrased language, write it down here in positively phrased language instead, adding as many specifics as possible.

I don't want	What do I want instead?

Example

I don't want to live in a polluted town any more. I currently live in a small flat in a noisy town with no greenery.

It is November 2008. I now live in a two-storey house in the countryside. There are fields on each side. The house has two bedrooms and two bathrooms. I own it and have fully paid off my mortgage.

✏️ What did I get last time?

One way to really get specific about what you want is to make a list of what you have manifested so far in your life in all the different areas.

Next, you can look at the list and decide what you would like to keep, and what you would like to get rid of. For everything that you want to get rid of, write down next to it what you want instead. From your new list, you can construct your cosmic order. You will have the opportunity to do this at the end of this chapter.

What have I manifested so far in this area?	**What do I want now?** (What do I want to get rid of and what do I want to keep?)
Example: Money	
I often have an overdraft and I have an outstanding debt to a friend.	*My bank account is always in credit, I have paid off all my debts and I have saved 10 per cent of my income this year.*

5: Check how much you really want what you're about to order

We have so many options nowadays. Should I be a banker or look after orphans in Africa? Should I write a book or be a gardener? Should I buy a car or a new sound system? Should I get married? Should I get divorced? Should I have children?

Why do you want what you want?

What do you think will change in your life as the result of having what you want – the new car, the new home, the new relationship, the new career, the sporting or business success?

Asking for something more than the material

Surely cosmic ordering is not just about presenting a long list of consumer-driven demands to the cosmos? Of course, you can ask for the new car or the new kitchen you want. If you do, you are very likely to get it.

But, many people when they place an order with the cosmos for a new car or kitchen are really seeking something bigger – a sense of purpose. They hope that all the things or experiences they ask for will give them something bigger – and fill a hole in their lives.

As we have said earlier, the old adage goes, be careful what you ask for, because you might, and surely will, get it.

We want everything we want for a reason. That reason is

always, without exception, linked to a feeling. Maybe you believe getting a new car will make you feel happy. Perhaps having children will bring you joy. What about money? What will you buy with it and what feeling will that give you more of?

Feeling that you have more purpose, fulfilment, enjoyment or happiness in your life will not come about by making a consumer choice. If by asking for a particular order you are really asking for – and this is nearly always the case – a feeling, you need to write this into your order.

The first step is to decide what feelings you want more of in your life.

Equally, it may be that you want to *avoid* a feeling. Perhaps a romantic relationship will help you to avoid the pain of loneliness? Maybe a new career will stop you feeling unsuccessful?

Check to see if there is a match between the feelings you want and the orders you place.

Ask yourself: 'Why is this important to me?'

Why do you want what you want? What will it give you more of? What will it allow you to be or do more of in your life?

Will what you have asked for really bring you what you think it will?

What are the big reasons why you want what you want? Here are some to start you thinking. Circle any that you relate to and add your own to the list.

Learning

Service

Love

Making the world a better place

Challenge

Freedom

Fulfilment

Self-reliance

Mastery

Playfulness   Creativity

Excitement   Safety

Security

Simplicity

Fun

Change

Joy

Happiness   Synergy   Harmony

Truth

Using my abilities

Wisdom   Zest for life

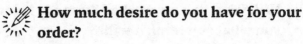 **How much desire do you have for your order?**

Every order and intention you send to the universe must have the force of energy behind it. Ask yourself: 'When my cosmic order is delivered, what feeling will this give me?'

Think about one of the dreams you have written down so far. Write down the feeling that you want more of in your life by having this dream fulfilled.

Dream

....

....

....

Why is it important to me?

....

....

....

What feeling do I want more of by asking for this?

....

....

....

FAQs

Is there a limit to the number of orders I can have at any one time?

The answer is No. You are sending out orders all the time anyway through your unconscious thoughts. The universe is abundant. It is like an enormous cosmic storehouse that can never be emptied. You can visualise every day being full of good things and good feelings and as long as you sincerely expect it to be so, you will transmit these orders out to the universe and every day really will be happy.

Can I ask for a bad thing to happen to someone else?

You can, but it will hurt you more than you hurt the other person. As the old saying goes, when you point one finger at someone there are three fingers pointing back at you. The rule of three is a universal karmic law – the natural justice system of the universe. If you wish one bad thing towards another person, you will get the bad energy back threefold.

Always set up the expectation that the universe will give you good feelings, in addition to what you want.

Each time you write down your cosmic order, say thank you in advance for all the good feelings that will now flow into your life. For example: 'Thank you for making my life enjoyable, happy and fun on a daily, regular and consistent basis.'

The universe will do everything to bring you those good feelings.

Dave's story:
The case of the perfect woman

After I got divorced I felt very bruised by the experience. I had a few flings and I really wanted to meet Miss Right, but I wasn't prepared to go through what I had gone through before. I decided to get very detailed. I wrote an exact 'job specification' out: what I wanted in the perfect woman – physical, emotional and mental characteristics. Because I am a vegetarian, I threw that in, too.

I didn't believe for a moment that this woman would even exist, but I am precise in my work so I thought I might as well get precise now. I started doing internet dating, but didn't meet anyone who matched up to my image.

Then one day I was standing in the post office queue and I bumped into a friend with his gorgeous new girlfriend. We got chatting and headed off for a drink. Then I discovered that she wasn't his girlfriend. But now she is mine – and she matched my list exactly.

Life lists

Now it's time to start making lists of cosmic orders for all areas of your life. You will use these worksheets as the basis for the next steps. The life areas below are important for most people; however, you can make extra worksheets to complete for areas of your own choosing. Take as many copies of each as you wish. Give yourself as much space as you need to be as detailed as possible.

Tip **Make a note**

It may be a good idea to write in pencil, or to take some photocopies of this list, as you may want to revise it or add to it as you go on.

Refer back to everything you have thought about and written down so far in the previous steps.

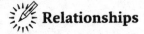 **Relationships**

What have I been, done, had in past relationships	My cosmic orders – what do I want now? (Write down what you want specifically, in the present tense using 'I'.)
Example **Been:** *I have been dishonest.* **Done:** *I have broken promises in my relationships and not said what I want.* **Had:** *I have had short relationships.*	*I am now in a happy, on-going relationship where we have committed to each other and are open and honest in our communication; for example, we say we love each other and say when we are vulnerable or upset.*

Why is this important to me?	What feeling do I want more of by asking for this?	How will my life change when I get this?
It is important for me to share my feelings with someone, and to have long-term companionship and love.	*Love, joy, happiness.*	*I will learn to share more, to commit and will have dealt with my fears about honest communication.*

Career

What have I been, done, had in my past career(s)	My cosmic orders – what do I want now? (Write down what you want specifically, in the present tense using 'I'.)
Example **Been:** *I was hard-working.* **Done:** *I gave all my energy to my career and neglected my home life.* **Had:** *I had great financial success.*	*I am now in a career where I work three days a week for half my existing salary.*

Why is this important to me?	What feeling do I want more of by asking for this?	How will my life change when I get this?
To give me energy for other parts of my life.	*Energy and excitement for my social life and passion for what I love.*	*I will have satisfaction in all parts of my life.*

Suzanna's story:
The case of the part-time job

I made a big decision after my last job that I wasn't going to get burnt out any more. I wanted a new job but with decent money. I still had a big mortgage to pay.

I went looking for part-time project manager jobs, but of course there weren't any. Then a friend gave me an intro to a very high-powered company. I asked him if it was likely I could go part-time. He said absolutely not. Still, I decided to take the interview because it had been so long since I'd had one, I needed the practice.

The interview went well. We even got to the salary discussion point. I asked for a huge amount of money – double my previous salary – and told them (because I didn't care at this point) that I had already been offered more than this for three days a week at another company. They seemed impressed.

At this point I dared to raise the dreaded words 'part-time'. As I suspected, the interviewer didn't seem interested. Then out of the blue, it was as if a light bulb was suddenly going off inside his head.

'How about four days a week,' he said? 'Of course, I would have to offer you 20 per cent less than what we discussed. The thing is, one of our staff in our other office really wants to cut down her hours because she is looking after her elderly mother, but we can't let her go because it is one of our most important jobs. Would you be okay with working two miles further away?'

Of course I was, and I ended up in a small, friendly office, job sharing with a fantastic woman.

Janet's story:
The case of the six-figure salary

A few years ago I was working in the human resources department of a financial company in Northern England. I knew I wanted a change and a promotion, but even though I applied for several jobs nothing happened.

Then I discovered cosmic ordering. I visualised a new job. I was really clear about what I wanted – a director-level job in the same area. I imagined what it would be like to be in my new position. I saw myself in my swish new office, sitting in my chair talking to people as the director of the department. I could hear what they were saying and I could even feel in my imagination what it felt like – really exciting!

I imagined myself in my new job in a month's time. I saw it as if it was a big cross sitting in the middle of a line going out from my present to my future. Then, just for fun, as I visualised all of this, I decided to double my income from £50,000 to £100,000. I didn't really expect to get it, even though I knew that some really senior people in my field did get that kind of salary.

Three weeks later, out of the blue a head-hunter gave me a call. He offered me an interview for a job in the City of London as the director of HR at a big insurance company.

At the interview they asked me what salary I was expecting. I didn't have a clue so I fudged it and didn't really give an answer. The next day the head-hunter rang me. 'They are offering you the job,' he said, 'but they are a bit worried about the salary – is £100,000 enough?'

Money

What have I been, done, had in relation to money in the past	My cosmic orders – what do I want now? (Write down what you want specifically, in the present tense using 'I'.)
Example **Been:** *I was negligent about looking after my financial affairs and lost money.* **Done:** *I spent recklessly.* **Had:** *I had lots of money and wasted it.*	*I am now in control of my finances. I check my bank statements regularly. I make good investments. I make a salary of £30,000 a year and save £200 a month.*

Why is this important to me?	What feeling do I want more of by asking for this?	How will my life change when I get this?
To be responsible, rich and know that the money I have works for me – building up savings and a pension for my future.	*Happiness and calmness.*	*I will be more in control of all parts of my life – because I will have learnt how to pay attention to what matters.*

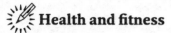 **Health and fitness**

What have I been, done, had in relation to health and fitness in the past	My cosmic orders – what do I want now? (Write down what you want specifically, in the present tense using 'I'.)
Example **Been:** *I have been lazy.* **Done:** *I did intermittent exercise every few months.* **Had:** *I had some good results when I did exercise. I changed my body shape and lost about 5 kg.*	*I am now fit and toned. I weigh 54 kg with a Body Mass Index of 21. I do exercise three times a week by going to the gym twice a week and jogging at the weekends.*

Why is this important to me?	What feeling do I want more of by asking for this?	How will my life change when I get this?
To stay healthy my entire life. To be the size and shape I want to be and maintain this.	*Vitality.*	*I will have lots of energy and feel great. That will keep me feeling good at work, and be positive for my sex life and relationship.*

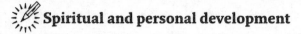# Spiritual and personal development

What have I been, done, had in my past spiritual and personal development	My cosmic orders - what do I want now? (Write down what you want specifically, in the present tense using 'I'.)
Example **Been:** *I have always been interested in my own development.* **Done:** *I have spent time on courses that I hoped would develop me and have had some positive results.* **Had:** *When I turned 30 I had some big leaps in my spiritual understanding.*	*I am now taking part in a regular spiritual development group, meeting once a week, in which we practise meditation and discuss life's big issues.*

Why is this important to me?	What feeling do I want more of by asking for this?	How will my life change when I get this?
To grow and develop as a human being.	*Fulfilment, self-love, bliss.*	*I will see life from a new perspective, know what is important, and find it easy to make decisions about what aspects of my life to keep and what to change.*

Summary Step 3

- Be specific about what you want to order. What do you intend to come into your life? What do you want to be, do, or have in your life?
- When do you want this?
- The more specific you are about what you want, the easier it will be for the cosmic storehouse to fulfil your order.
- Remember to write it down using personal and positively phrased language. If you can only think of what you don't want, ask yourself: 'What do I want instead of this?'
- Why do I want this? What will I be, do or have more of in my life by having the cosmos deliver this order to me?
- What feelings do I want more of by having this?
- How much do I want this?

Step 4:
Take charge of your thoughts

'*We do not see things as they are, we see them as we are.*'

THE TALMUD

You get what you focus on

Have you ever come across the serial dieter? You know her, don't you? She has a slow metabolism. She diets, but never loses a pound. Occasionally she loses a few pounds, but then puts them straight on again. It must be my genes, she says.

Over the years she has become extremely careful about what she eats, which means it is not very exciting to go out for a meal with her. She won't eat anything but low-calorie food. No sugar, no fat, no carbohydrates. Recently she has started to cut out fruit because of all the sugars. She has tried the Atkins and low-GI diets to no avail.

What's really going on? Remember, this is a thought universe. She believes so strongly she will get fat easily that she is attracting fat to her without even realising it. She is thinking about food the whole time and instead of eating less she actually eats more unintentionally. Her thin friend never thinks of the idea of getting fat and so actually eats less even though she never diets.

What about your other friend – the accident-prone one. She always goes out for an evening dressed up to the nines. But she invariably ends up with a big beetroot stain on her new white suit. Or she trips on the pavement and the heel of her shoe is left behind. She loses her purse in restaurants, she forgets her ticket for the train, she spills her coffee and she walks into doors. 'I am Miss Clumsy,' she says. 'My parents always told me that and they have been proved right. Look, last time I went out on a date, I accidentally knocked a bowl of soup all over the poor guy, then when I went to sponge him down, his glasses fell off, I stepped back and trod on them – I attract so much bad luck. I am bad at relationships, too'.

Remember, the Law of Attraction is, you get what you focus on. The only solution for these two women would be to change their focus.

Always focus on what you want.

Change your thoughts and change your life

Thought controls the universe. The universe is thought.

Every thought that comes from us attracts an immediate result. It is as if we are an invisible radio transmitter sending out signals to the mind of the universe. The second we think something, it attracts energy towards us.

If you believe you will put on weight, you will. If you believe you will be sick if you eat a certain food, you will. If you believe you can't sleep when it is noisy, of course you won't be able to.

In this Step we take a look at how you can clear a path in your unconscious for your order to be heard by the universe. By clearing out any thoughts that don't match with the order you are placing, you create a clear pathway for the transmission of your order to the universe.

Taking control

You should have total control over one thing in life – your thoughts. To summarise what Napoleon Hill wrote in his best-selling book *Think and Grow Rich*, it's okay to be careless with your possessions but not with your thoughts, because these are the means by which you control your future.

You can probably immediately think of friends or acquaintances who have beliefs about themselves which you know are blocking their chances for success and happiness.

But what about you?

Each of us sees life from a unique perspective. What you believe determines what events you attract. As your beliefs change, so does the world around you. Your beliefs create your reality.

As soon as you change your thoughts, no matter how much of a failure you think this is, you can instantly sow the seeds of success and begin to shape your future.

In fact, if you were to look back at every past positive change you have ever made in your life, you will notice that the amount of change is in *direct* proportion to a corresponding change in your thinking.

Pam's story:
The case of the wrong mansion

I live in America. I am coming up to retirement now. I have worked ever since I left school. I have travelled all over the world and I have gone from a tiny one-bedroom flat to living with my husband in a mansion. I always wanted to own a big property, but even though I live in this beautiful home I still feel that I don't have a property, because my husband insists that our house is kept entirely in his name.

What I realise is that I always had the belief when I was young that a nice girl should find a husband who would look after her and provide a home. I never developed the belief that I could do it on my own.

What you sow with your thoughts you reap with your subsequent circumstances.

Even though a seed disappears underground and is hidden in the soil for many weeks or months before the first shoots burst through, the planting of the seed leads directly to the flower that subsequently blossoms all that time later.

Likewise, there is a relationship between everything we *do* and what happens to us later. There is also the same relationship between what we *think* and what happens subsequently.

> *You can only believe what you can conceive.*
> *You can only achieve what you believe.*

In other words, be careful what you think because it will come true. Or, to take another way of thinking about this is, you can only achieve what you can conceive and believe. The implications for cosmic ordering are vital.

How to sabotage or assist your order

If you don't get your order delivered to you exactly as you have set it out, it may well be that you don't believe deep down that you can or should have this particular order.

Your cosmic order will *always* be as successfully delivered as you believe it can be. If you believe you can be rich and you ask for a lot of money to come into your life, the cosmos will deliver it. However, if you want to be rich but believe that you are destined to be poor, you may block your cosmic order with that thought.

'Well,' you might say, 'I *do* believe I can be rich and I have asked for more money and nothing has happened. I think about being rich all the time.'

On one level that's probably true – you do think that you believe this. But the blocking thought isn't necessarily the thought that you are consciously aware of. The thoughts that help us or set up obstacles to our goals are often our core beliefs, hidden deeply in our unconscious minds.

FAQ

Does cosmic ordering do away with the idea of a divine plan or destiny?

No, these two ideas may seem at first glance to be in opposition to each other, but many ancient religions and philosophies encompass both ideas – that we co-create with God/the universe; in other words, we have free will and choice and at the same time there is a big picture/divine plan for each of us that we have set up before we are born to help us grow and develop as human beings. This is similar to an idea often cited in astrology that the planets 'impel' but do not 'compel'. We are free to discover and experiment with life by ourselves and we have already set up the best overall conditions for us to develop spiritually. In other words, the universe will throw us situations that help us to develop as people and also allow us to determine our own choices of how to respond to these situations – that is, allow us free will.

Your powerful unconscious mind

The unconscious, or subconscious, mind is an amazing force. It has been called the powerhouse of the body. Just as the crew of a great cruise liner work seamlessly below decks making sure the ship always stays on course, the unconscious mind makes sure that your whole body runs like clockwork. It ensures that your blood keeps circulating, your organs carry out their functions, and every cell and atom inside you performs in accordance with their instructions.

You couldn't possibly perform these functions through conscious thought. The conscious mind would be overloaded within less than a second. Whereas the conscious mind can only cope with processing around seven bits of information per second, the unconscious mind has to cope with millions of bits of information hitting it in the same time frame.

Think for a moment of your lungs breathing. Until you saw those words you probably weren't even conscious of what they were doing. Now consider what it would be like if you had to think and tell every bit of your body what to do every second. Of course it would be impossible for you to function.

The unconscious mind also acts as a storehouse of every experience you have ever had. It stores away every situation you have ever seen, felt, heard, tasted or smelt as a memory and in a similar way it registers every single thought and belief that you have. It is like the most efficient video recorder you can imagine. The memories deep in your unconscious may never normally come to your conscious attention, but nevertheless they are always there as a great resource bank for you to access. If you have ever experienced hypnosis you will know that an old memory can suddenly come back in startling clarity once the unconscious mind is instructed to find it. Even though you are just thinking about this particular memory, you may experience it as if it is happening to you right now.

What this means is that if your memories are positive ones, they may support helpful beliefs that will enable you to get your cosmic orders. But if they are negative memories, you may well have formed beliefs about yourself that are not helpful in enabling you to get your order delivered.

The conscious captain

What, then, is the role of the conscious mind? The conscious mind is like the captain of a ship, giving directions for his crew to carry out. The crew's job is to follow instructions and so they will follow out your instructions to the letter just as long as your instructions are not in conflict with any other previous instructions they have received from you.

A conflict of instructions

Suppose that you place a cosmic order for a romantic relationship. You are absolutely convinced that you are ready for a relationship. You have a list of attributes that you wish the person to have. These include a stipulation that the man or woman should be financially secure. You know that you want this because every previous relationship you have had has fallen apart because of your partner's overspending. You place your order and a few weeks later the cosmos sends you a new relationship. But lo and behold, your new partner has no money either. Why? As you placed the order, the doubt that you could have a relationship without the problems of the old ones tainted your order. The unconscious heard your instruction for a new relationship and at the same time registered another instruction – your deep unconscious belief: 'I always attract relationships where my partner overspends.' So, following the principles of the Law of Attraction, it duly presented you with a match for the stronger instruction – the deep unconscious belief.

Here's an example. A woman wants a new career. She has just been made redundant from her old job and now she is worried. 'I am too old at 50 and I don't have a degree. No one will want to hire someone like me.' She sets up a cosmic order for a new job and an interview materialises out of nowhere. A friend of a friend suggests that she might be ideal for a position in his company. This is the cosmos directly presenting her with delivery of her order. But when she goes to the interview, she goes with the assumption that they will find her too old and undereducated. She assumes she will fail the interview and sure enough her self-fulfilling prophecy comes true. Misinterpreting the body language of the interviewer as being hostile to her, she flunks the interview.

What about other areas of life? Peter desperately wants to be healthy. Every time you speak to him he talks about how ill he is. He has Chronic Fatigue Syndrome and believes that it is getting worse. It is important to him to prove he has it because he is relying for income on benefits and medical insurance. The doctors aren't convinced that he is ill because they can't find any hard evidence by testing him as to what is going on, even though it is clear he has to sleep far longer than an average person. Peter is getting more and more annoyed by the attitude of everyone around him and has started to keep a diary of his symptoms. In fact, during his waking hours, he spends a lot of time each day focusing on all the specific things that may prove to the insurance company, benefits assessors and doctors that he has a real illness that they 'should do something about'. At the same time, though, he is clear that the biggest goal in his life is to get better. He wants to be up and about again and feeling healthy. But when he placed a cosmic order for good health, nothing happened.

Why? One thing is clear, he spends more time with pictures in his mind of being ill than of being healthy. Every day he is focusing on how he can prove to the world at large that his tiredness is not an illusion. The thought that he must prove to everyone the reason for his symptoms is far stronger than the focus he has on the possibility of getting better. Of course, he wants to be healthy, but he also admits he would be annoyed if he became healthy again before he had proved he was ill and had to say to the doctors 'I am no longer ill'. Currently his investment in being right is stronger than his investment in being healthy.

How to find out what thoughts may block your cosmic order

Here are some more common unhelpful beliefs that people have about themselves:

- I am not a lucky person
- I don't deserve to be happy/rich/have fun
- I am fated to have the life I have
- I can be poor or happy

- Everyone gets ill when they're old
- People get lonely as they get older
- If I say what I want, I will be rejected/look silly
- I am not fated to be successful
- I can't choose my life. I have too many responsibilities
- I can't hold down a job for more than a few months
- I am bad at relationships
- I am too nice to succeed
- I am not good enough
- I am not lovable
- Other people are better than me

Do you have any ideas like these about yourself? Any such beliefs could act as self-sabotage for a cosmic order.

Beliefs that sabotage your cosmic orders

Let's take a look at your beliefs.

It is no point saying, 'I want a happy relationship,' if you believe, 'I am bad at relationships' or even, 'I can only hold down a relationship for a few months'.

However, if you believe, 'I am very good at relationships' or, 'my relationships always last until I want to end them' these beliefs will match your want.

It is not unusual to hold mixed thoughts about the same subject. For example, 'I am good at starting relationships, but I tend to pick the wrong people'. Or, 'I am good at putting energy into relationships, but if I am in a relationship I might feel stuck'.

You often see these mixed beliefs in yo-yo dieters. When you consistently lose weight and then put it on again, there are probably some mixed beliefs in there – for example, 'I want to lose weight. I know that eating less means that people lose weight. But I also believe that if I lose weight I will attract more attention and I am uncomfortable with that.'

Before you place any order for what you want, it is essential that you identify what your beliefs are, so that if they are beliefs that will sabotage your order you can change them to beliefs that match the order you are about to place.

How to change sabotaging beliefs

You can do this in two stages:

 Firstly, by brainstorming every blocking belief that you may have about what you want.

 Then, to begin to think about any conflicting beliefs you may hold that might be equally, or even more, valid (see pages 113–114).

We're going to start by looking at a few different ways you can tweak your unconscious beliefs out of your unconscious mind. These exercises will identify what beliefs you hold that make up your view of the world and assess whether any of them are limiting you in any way or stopping you from realising your dreams.

Belief brainstorming

The way to get at your beliefs is with simple brainstorming exercises.

 To begin, relax and turn your attention towards yourself. You might want to take a few deep breaths just to compose yourself and to still your mind.

2 Imagine you can shine a big spotlight into your unconscious mind, or reach inside to the place where all your unconscious beliefs are held. Take a look at what's in there. As you do this, remember you are doing this for you. Whatever you find inside, whatever you write down about your findings, you can let go of what other people might think about you and just be really honest with yourself. After all, the more you can identify what thoughts have held you back in the past, or what thoughts hold you back now, the more quickly you can move forward towards your dreams from this moment on.

 3 Whatever you write down, read it without judgement. Look at what you have written as if it has no emotional significance for you. Notice what you are thinking and begin to question why you think in that way.

The more you can challenge your limiting beliefs dispassionately, the more your world, life, behaviour and experiences will change as a result. Even shifting one core belief will lead to the adjusting of many more beliefs that have clustered around it.

For example, if you were to challenge an 'I am' belief such as 'I am not lovable', you would have an effect not just on one part of your life but probably many more. It is like undoing a stitch in a piece of knitting. Taking out one stitch causes the rest of the knitting to unravel.

What do you really believe about yourself?

Try the following exercise.

 1 Look back at your Life Lists in Step 3 (see pages 74–85).

For each list, take a look at the 'What have I been, done, had' column.

 Think about what you have created in your life up to now and ask yourself the question, 'What do I believe about myself that has led to me creating this situation?' In other words, do you believe anything about yourself that has helped you in your life in the past, but is now holding you back?

For example, in the area of romantic relationships, suppose that you had written: *'I have attracted a partner who can't say he loves me.'* What would you have (had) to believe about yourself to create this situation?

Maybe your answer would be: *'I don't believe that I am lovable.'*

Or perhaps: *'I believe that if someone declares his/her love then it means that I might have to say it back and secretly I am not sure I want to.'*

Or, in the area of finance: *'I never have enough money.'* What would you have (had) to believe about yourself to create this situation?

How about: *'I don't believe I am worth more money.'*

'I believe it is not possible to have the money I want and do what I love.'

'I believe if I had more money I would have to be more responsible in my life.'

These are just examples. Your beliefs will be unique and personal to you. However, beliefs are not permanent. As you clarify your beliefs about the different areas of your life, remember, as soon as you become conscious of what your beliefs are, you can change them.

Your expectations: 'shoulds', 'musts' and 'have to's'

What do you believe that you should do? Must be? Or have to do, be, or have in your life? What would happen if you didn't believe this?

Your expectations about yourself and the world are closely aligned to your beliefs. Your 'shoulds', 'musts' and 'have to's' come from what you have been told by others in your childhood, your peer group and by society. They are the ways in which you try to please other people by buying into the ideal image they have created.

If you have other people's expectations of yourself and your life in your head, it only fuels disappointment and frustration. Even when you get what you think you want, you find you never really wanted it. Or you find you can never live up to someone else's expectations and, falling short, you try again and replace the old expectations with a different set of new expectations, without feeling any sense of satisfaction.

You can choose right now to discard this idealised image and get back to the real you. Yes, this may cause you to change your mind about some of the things you thought that you wanted. If so, go back and revise your list.

The exercise below is an opportunity to get all your 'shoulds', 'musts' and 'have to's' onto paper and to reveal some of the unconscious beliefs you have about yourself.

✎ 'Shoulds', 'musts' and 'have to's'

I believe that I should always:
Example
Be nice to everyone for them to like me.

I believe that I must:
Work hard to succeed.

I believe that I have to:
Agree with my partner if I am to keep my relationship.

I believe that man should always:
Be in charge.

I believe that a man must:
Be macho to succeed.

I believe that a man has to:
Earn more than a woman.

I believe that a woman should always:
Look good to have a relationship.

I believe that a woman must:
Be slim to be loved.

I believe that a woman has to:
Stay looking good her whole life long.

Now, think about life, yourself as a whole, and then each area of your life in turn. Jot down some thoughts.

What do you want instead of your 'shoulds', 'musts' and 'have to's'?

ME AND LIFE AS A WHOLE
Example
I believe that I should always be nice to people for them to like me.

Instead
I want to communicate my feelings honestly in all my relationships.

HEALTH AND FITNESS

Instead

CAREER

_____

Instead

_____

_____

MONEY

_____

Instead

_____

_____

RELATIONSHIPS

_____

Instead

_____

_____

Tip **Take your time**

It is tempting to rush so that you can get through to the Magic Formula at the end of the book, but the more time you spend on this the more good things will come into your life. Spend some time with yourself now for a big pay-off later.

⚡ Life beliefs

Take some time once again to review your Life Lists as a starting point for your thinking. You may well be able to think of other beliefs that you hold about yourself once you get started.

Write down anything and everything that comes to mind – it doesn't matter if they are positive or negative beliefs. In fact, you may be pleasantly surprised just how many positive beliefs you do hold about yourself. Use the worksheet below and make extra copies if necessary.

What do I believe about life?

What would I have (had) to believe about myself to create my life as it is right now?

Positive beliefs
I believe...

_____

_____

_____

_____

I don't believe...

_____

_____

_____

How can these positive beliefs help me get what I want?

Limiting beliefs
I believe...

I don't believe...

How are these limiting beliefs stopping me from getting what I want in my life?

Now repeat this exercise for specific areas of your life:

- What do I believe about myself?
- What do I believe about myself and my romantic relationships?
- What do I believe about my career?
- What do I believe about money?

- What do I believe about spiritual growth?
- What do I believe about personal development?
- What do I believe about my social life?
- What do I believe about myself and my family?
- What do I believe about myself and my home?

Look at the belief list you have written down and think about what you have said you want in terms of cosmic orders. How well do the beliefs you have written down match the orders? Do the beliefs you have support the expectation that your orders will be delivered? Are there any beliefs that you need to change so that you can really believe that you deserve to and will get everything you dream of having in your life?

How to change your beliefs

You can change any habit – or indeed any aspect of your life – within a very short space of time, often less than a month. This series of exercises will loosen up all your self-limiting beliefs so that you can begin to choose thoughts that match your cosmic orders.

Creating a positive memory bank

The first exercise is a way for you to change the script in your mind. If your life story were to be made into a film right now, what kind of film would it be? A drama, a comedy, a tragedy, a thriller, perhaps an exciting adventure? Would it have a happy ending? Would it have love scenes? Would there be times of great happiness that made the audience wish that they were living the main character's life?

We script our own lives. Our memory is selective. Whatever has happened to us, bad or good, we choose what we focus on. What we choose to focus on impacts upon our beliefs about who we are, the life we are leading, and the life we can choose to lead from now on.

By changing the script inside your head to the most positive one you can write, you will change your beliefs about yourself at the same time, and build an expectation of good things happening to you. You will create a positive memory bank as a foundation for all the new beliefs you are going to gain.

Creating a positive memory bank is a powerful way of feeding your unconscious positive feelings.

 To begin, let your mind look back over your past. However, as you do this deliberately search for the positive memories. It doesn't matter how small or big the memory you can find first of all, simply let your mind be selective and latch on to any positive picture, feeling, sound or other sensation, even if it is only for a few seconds.

 If you catch sight of something negative, deliberately blur the picture in your brain. Imagine you can turn down the brightness and make it look dark and dull. Or see what happens to how you feel about it if you shrink the picture.

 If you don't have a picture but you do have a negative emotion or sound, immediately imagine that you can turn down the feeling or volume. Picture a dial inside you that allows you to reduce the sensation. Imagine that the numbers run from 0 to 10 with 10 as the strongest sensation. What is the strength of feeling/volume at present? Note it, and turn the dial until you reduce the numbers. You can repeat this however many times are needed to bring the dial permanently down to zero.

4 Now pick out a pleasant memory. Remember it in as much detail as possible. See it like a film running on a screen in front of you. Deliberately turn up the brightness and colour on the film so that it becomes as vivid as possible. You may also find you want to make it bigger in your imagination, or bring objects in the film closer to you. You can revisit this pleasant memory and make adjustments to your enjoyment of the film as often as you wish.

5 Now picture your dial again. You can use the dial to bring good feelings and pleasant sounds into your experience of this memory. Take a note of what number the dial is currently set on. Turn the dial up. You can repeat this as many times as you like by revisiting the memory until the dial is permanently set on 10. With each number, your enjoyment of the feelings and/or sounds associated with the memory will increase.

Repeat this process with as many memories as possible every day over the next month and you will find that your brain will build a new habit and remember your past in a positive light.

Why it is important for you to change your beliefs

Before you can change your beliefs permanently, it is important to check just how committed you are to changing your existing beliefs. Every belief you hold currently exists because it brings a positive benefit to your life – you will start to hold new beliefs only at the point when you can convince your unconscious mind that the new belief will bring you as many benefits as the old one.

To begin, choose one of the beliefs that you have written down in the previous exercises.

A belief is just an opinion. It is not a fact. We believe it is a fact because we accumulate evidence to support our beliefs all the time. That's why people can become more fixed about what they believe as they get older.

Jane Roberts, author of *The Nature of Personal Reality*, says that it is useful to think of beliefs as old furniture. You can change your furniture, you can rearrange it, or you can get rid of it. It doesn't control you.

If you were to 'redecorate' your life now, how many of your old beliefs would you throw out and how many would you keep?

Tip **Ordering up good health**

If you have a complex health problem, it is vital to spend enough time on investigating what beliefs you currently hold so that you can get a picture of yourself in perfect health, 100 per cent free of any doubt. If necessary when you set up your order, make a number of interim orders for stages of improvement so that you can convince yourself adequately along the way that the process is working – this will boost your belief power.

Challenging your old beliefs

The following exercise takes any belief that you have identified so far and challenges it. After recognising that your belief is simply an opinion, you have the choice to decide what you would like to believe instead.

It doesn't matter if at this point you don't believe 100 per cent in the evidence for these new beliefs. You simply want to shake your current beliefs up a bit and loosen up your thinking, so that you allow a new thought to form.

Tip **Record new evidence**

It is very important that you write down any evidence for a new belief that you can think of so that it seems as solid to the unconscious as your old beliefs.

Your new beliefs don't have to be *probable* at this point, only *possible*. However, the best way to begin to believe your new beliefs is to start actively to look for evidence that they might indeed be true.

 What I want, what I believe, what I can believe instead

Here's an example of how to begin to challenge your thoughts.

What do I want?
A job I love for which I am paid 50 per cent more than I am at present and in the town I live in. I want to maintain a balance between my home and work life and work the same number of hours as I do now.

My current beliefs about this want
There aren't any highly paid jobs in this town for people like me.

Challenging my thoughts – a new belief
There may be highly paid people working in this town that I haven't met. It is a large town after all.

Evidence that my new belief may be true
I have heard that my neighbour earns a lot of money.

Now it's your turn:

What do I want?

....

....

....

My current beliefs about this want

Challenging my thoughts – a new belief

Evidence that my new belief may be true

My new beliefs about myself and my life that will support me in having, doing and being what I want:

Keep on looking for and accumulating evidence to support your new beliefs. As you work through the rest of the book, keep a note of any new, positive and empowering beliefs that occur to you. Refer back to this list at any time you want reassurance that you are on track in your cosmic ordering.

✏️ Changing your present beliefs – choosing a belief role model

Think of an area of your life where you feel that you are not on track currently. You are going to choose a role model. This can be someone you know, or have read about, or can imagine.

Start by asking yourself:

Does anyone I know, or have heard of, or can imagine, already have what I want in this area?

....

....

....

....

Who are they?

....

....

....

....

> **What beliefs do I think they must hold about themselves and life in general to have created their current circumstances?**
>
> _____
>
> _____
>
> _____
>
> **Having seen the benefits their empowering beliefs produce, which of these beliefs could I now adopt?**
>
> _____
>
> _____
>
> _____

It doesn't matter that you are using your imagination in this exercise; this makes it even more convincing for your unconscious mind. It is a great way for you to work out what beliefs will achieve the results you want.

> **Changing your present beliefs – three thank yous**
>
> Finally, this is an exercise to keep you on track in your thoughts. Doing this exercise will increase your luck in life and boost your emotional state. It is particularly useful to do if you are not good yet at keeping totally

positive on a daily basis. It will help you to tune into all the gifts you are already receiving from the universe.

Over the next month, each day try to write down at least three things you are thankful for. These can be anything at all, small or large – for example, someone opening a door for you, receiving a happy phone call from a friend, or simply realising how happy you are to be alive and healthy.

(Make as many copies of this sheet as you need to.)

Date:

Thank you for:

Date:

Thank you for:

Date:

Thank you for:

Creating a third act

The next worksheet is for you to use to begin the process of thinking about what beliefs you would like to have in your positive future memory bank. Doing this exercise will stimulate your creativity and imagination as well as providing a further check on whether what you have written down so far is what you really want for your future.

✎ Remember your old script. It's time to write a new one.

Think about your story so far – the story with all the positive memories in it. Suppose you have already lived the first and second acts, what will your third act be like?

Write down a brief paragraph describing what your future life will look like. Will it be full of laughter, happiness, adventure, excitement, learning, love? All of the above? What will it look like, sound like, feel like?

_____

_____

_____

_____

_____

_____

Now look back at your Life Lists on pages 74–85. Knowing what you now know about what you want your future to be like, what can you add to your lists to ensure your future is what you really want it to be?

Summary Step 4

- How much do I believe that I can have my order delivered to me just as I have asked for it?
- Remember that you can begin to choose your own thoughts. What you believe is the key to what you can manifest.
- Other people's thoughts belong to them. Get rid of the 'shoulds', 'musts' and 'have to's'.
- What are your beliefs about what you want? Do you believe you can have it?
- What new beliefs do you want to have? What is the evidence that your new beliefs rather than your old beliefs might be true?

Step 5:
Access your inner power

'For every man the world is as fresh
As it was at the first day,
And as full of untold novelties
For him who has the eyes to see them.'

THOMAS HENRY HUXLEY

How to access your inner power

Inside yourself you have all the resources you could ever need to change your life in any way you want. You are a powerful individual with access to complete self-knowledge about what you can do with your life and how to attract it to you. You don't have to ask anyone else. Everything you need to know, you already know.

In this Step you will learn how to increase your power to access these resources easily and effortlessly on a daily basis.

The alpha state

The most powerful way to access your inner power is to relax to the extent that you reach a trance-like state. The way you can do this is through relaxation, meditation and deep, rhythmic breathing.

When you relax, your brain waves slow down to what is known as the alpha state, or even the deeper theta state. When you go about your day-to-day activities you habitually drift between the beta state (where the brain has electrical activity of between 13 and 30 cycles per second) and the alpha state (where the brain activity slows to around 7 and 13 cycles per second). In the theta state the brain slows to between 4 and 7 cycles per second.

When you relax deeply, or meditate either just through focusing on slowing your body, or through deep, regular breathing, you can slow your brain down easily to the alpha level. You may even find that you can relax even more deeply and dip in and out of the theta level. The alpha and theta levels of relaxation are the levels at which you enter a state known as a meditative or trance state. If you have ever been to see a hypnotherapist or tried self-hypnosis, you will have experienced this state during the process.

There are two reasons to practise being in a relaxed, trance state. In this Step you will explore both of these.

Firstly, being deeply relaxed enables you to reach that perfect state from where you can connect through your unconscious with the cosmic mind and receive guidance from your higher self about all aspects of your cosmic order; this includes inspiration about what you really want and guidance as to how to overcome any blocks or obstacles. When you relax to the alpha level, your conscious mind gets out of the way and a clear path of communication is cleared to your unconscious.

Secondly, a relaxed state is the best place from which to visualise your cosmic order. By practising visualisation from an alpha state, you can become adept at making detailed pictures of your order. This is essential preparation for *Step 6: Place your order*.

In our day-to-day activities we don't always stay in the moment. Our attention and focus can be all over the place as our conscious mind is continually distracting us with thoughts about little niggles or problems. In the meditative or trance alpha state, you are able to focus and visualise for a sustained length of time because the mind is stiller and calmer than it is during the everyday beta state. The more you can see in your mind's eye what you want, the more accurate the cosmos can be in what it delivers.

Accessing inner guidance

Inner guidance or intuition is the process of acquiring accurate information by bypassing your logical and conscious mind. Intuition is a sudden flash, deep insight, gut feeling, or *knowing*. It is akin to genius. It can let us know when something is wrong, or when it is absolutely right. It can tell us who to spend time with, what career to follow, how to make money or how to be safe. This inner guidance is unrelated to reason and so many of us, especially in Western society, get used to ignoring it, or denying it. But your inner guidance is the best way you have to make sure that you are on track and are asking for what will really bring happiness into your life.

To access your inner guidance, it is important to learn how to go easily into the relaxed state we call the trance, meditative, or alpha state. You can be directed into a trance state by another person (for example, a hypnotist), or access the state by yourself. The following exercise shows you how to enter and recognise a trance state yourself.

Accessing a deeply relaxed state

When you first start, practise accessing a relaxed alpha-level state for anything between five minutes and half an hour. The more you practise the more proficient you will become at relaxing quickly. And the more you practise being in this relaxed, trance-like state the longer you are likely to maintain it, because it feels so enjoyable.

 Sit or lie down. Choose somewhere where you can maintain the same position with comfort, remembering that you are going to remain in the same position for a while. Make sure that you won't be disturbed. Take the phone off the hook, close the door and choose a quiet place. When you get used to relaxing, it won't matter what background noise or disturbances there are as you will be able to attain your relaxed state in any circumstances.

 Make sure that your clothing is comfortable. Allow your arms to rest either in your lap or by your side. If you are sitting in a chair, keep your legs firmly rested and supported on the ground and parallel.

 Close your eyes. See how slowly you can open them. Then shut them and open them again, but twice as slowly as before. Notice that your eyelids reach a point where they are glued in place by the feeling of relaxation as if the muscles just won't work any more.

 With your eyes still closed, roll your eyes up inside your head as if looking at your eyebrows. You will feel as if your eyes are straining a little as you do this. As soon as this happens it means that you are beginning to activate and access your alpha brain waves. Relax.

 Now take a deep breath in, hold it for a count of 10 and then let the breath out. Take another breath, hold it for 10 and then exhale. Take another breath in the same way and then a third, so that you begin to feel your breath slowing down. As you breathe more and more deeply, you will begin to feel your whole body relaxing as if waves of relaxation are flowing from the top of your head right down to your toes.

Become aware of each part of your body becoming heavier. Starting at the top of your head, notice how heavy your head feels, then your neck. Let go of all the tension in your head and neck and let your head flop.

7 Now feel the relaxation sweep down from your head through your shoulders and arms, feeling them becoming heavy and relaxed. Release any tension from this area and feel the relaxation as if the top of your body is becoming light and floaty.

8 Next, become aware of your torso and stomach. Feel the relaxation flow throughout this part of your body as you release any tension. It feels almost as if you have a shower of relaxation pouring down your body and washing away all the little stresses in the muscles.

9 Become aware of your legs and feet. Allow the waves of relaxation to flow into this part of your body. Feel your legs and feet releasing all their tension into the air around you, and becoming light. Now your whole body will feel light and floaty.

10 Next, deepen your level of relaxation. Imagine in your mind's eye that there are ten steps in front of you going down. Hold the picture in your mind and begin to count backwards from 10 to 1 as you imagine yourself moving down the steps one at a time. With every step downwards, you increase your feelings of deep relaxation. You can deepen this feeling of relaxation even further by not simply seeing the steps but imagining that you can feel the steps beneath your feet, and hear your feet as they touch each step.

11 At the bottom of the steps you can see a door. Go through it. Behind the door you step into a place of relaxation: this may be a peaceful room with a bed to lie down on, it could be a beach where you can lie on the sand, or a soft lawn in the countryside, or any other peaceful place that you can picture in your mind's eye. Rest and relax in this place for however long you want. Enjoy what you see, hear and feel in this place. You are fully in your relaxed alpha- or theta-level state now.

 Whenever you want to come out of this state of relaxation, simply count upwards from 1 to 5 in your mind.

- At the count of 1, leave the place you are in and close the door behind you.
- At the count of 2, begin to increase your breathing.
- At the count of 3, allow the breath to begin to awaken your body.
- At the count of 4, begin to become aware of your body again. Say to yourself, 'When I open my eyes, I will be feeling alert and wonderful.'
- At the count of 5, open your eyes.

 Notice how you feel, take your time and get up slowly.

As you become more familiar with accessing this relaxed alpha-level state, you will find that it won't be necessary to take so long to relax your mind and body. Your unconscious will have become so used to the process of going into this meditative state that you can take yourself down very quickly just by closing your eyes, taking a few breaths and relaxing your mind and body.

FAQ

How will I know that I am at the alpha level?

Being at the alpha level simply feels like a pleasant state of relaxation in which time seems to be passing at a different rate than in the 'normal' beta state. You may feel yourself going in and out of this state naturally in everyday life: for example, when you are engrossed in watching a film or television programme. Time distortion is one of the most recognisable indicators. At these moments, time appears to pass more quickly or slowly than normal. You may even have the sensation of having lost time.

There are other indicators too. The body becomes still, so that it is easy to hold the same position for a long time. Breathing deepens and becomes slower. You will cease to notice noise and external distractions because your focus will be on what is happening internally. If you are watching someone else who is in this state, you'll see the muscles throughout their body relax. The person doesn't move very much. Even smaller movements in the body are stilled. When you look at the person's face, their mouth may appear to droop. If they speak, their voice sounds more relaxed and deeper than usual.

This is the level of relaxation that hypnotists use to give suggestions to the unconscious mind. In this state it becomes easy to access the resources of the unconscious mind, as you will see in the following exercises.

Contacting your inner guide

Do you believe in the existence of guardian angels or guides? If you do, you may already be used to asking your angel for help or guidance. Perhaps your name for such guidance is simply intuition. The meditation outlined below can help you access guidance from within, whether you believe that it comes from your own intuition or see it as a spiritual being that is there to take care of you. Let's call the place you go to for guidance your 'inner guide' – the voice inside you that can give you messages about what will bring you more joy.

 Sit quietly. Close your eyes. Feel the eyelids relax until the point where the muscles just won't work. With your eyes still closed, roll your eyes up inside your head as if you are looking at your eyebrows.

 Now take a deep breath in, hold it for a count of 10 and then let the breath out. Take another breath, hold it for 10 and then exhale. Take a third breath in the same way so that you begin to feel your breath slowing down. As you breathe more and more deeply, you will begin to feel your whole body relaxing as if waves of relaxation are flowing from the top of your head right down to your toes.

 Relax into your alpha state. You are going to enter a place of inner safety inside yourself. This is your personal sanctuary. In this place, you can experience feeling totally safe and secure. Imagine that you are looking out to a beautiful landscape in nature – your personal sanctuary. What is the first image that comes to mind? Wherever you choose, this will be the same place in which you contact your guide in future.

4 Notice what it feels like to be in this place of sanctuary. Feel the air on your face, the ground beneath your feet. Perhaps there are sounds too – birds singing, or a light breeze.

5 Find a place to sit amongst nature. State your intention. Invite your guide (or guides) to come to you.

6 There is a mist in front of you. Your guide is waiting for you behind the mist. Ask for your guide to appear to you. Become aware that your guide is approaching you.

7 Ask for the mist to clear and for your guide to be revealed to you. Ask to see your guide's shape. They may come in a human form, as an animal, or as any other shape.

8 Greet your guide. Perhaps they have a name? Or maybe this guide is simply called 'inner guidance', or 'intuition'.

9 Ask your guide if they are willing to communicate with you. If they say no, ask under what conditions would they be willing to communicate with you.

10 If they say yes, ask your guide for any special guidance, advice, or direction that they have for you at this point. You can ask your guide how he, she, or it usually likes to communicate with you.

11 The guidance may come in any form: as a flash of knowledge, a voice, or a feeling in your gut, or simply as a sense that you know what is right for you.

12 You may come back and ask further questions in future. If you wish to, invite your guide to stay with you to give you guidance about a particular issue. You can also ask your guide to give you guidance on a nightly basis through your dreams.

☼13☼ When you have finished, thank your guide with love. Watch your guide leave you and go back into the mist.

Asking for a life vision

Your guide can give you particular assistance with regard to issues such as an overall vision for your life. To ask about this area you can ask your guide:

- Please reveal to me any aspects of my life vision that will guide me at this point.
- What is my current role in relation to this life vision?
- What resources do I have within me now to keep me on the path to this vision?
- What beliefs do I have that are obstacles to me staying on the path to this vision?
- What beliefs do I have that will keep me on the path to this vision?

As you do this, notice what feelings are going on in your body. Ask:

- What steps can I take towards my life vision?
- What cosmic order would most guide me towards this life vision?

How to get in touch with your inner guide on a regular basis

As well as practising your inner guide exercise, it's good to get in touch with your sense of guidance and intuition during your everyday life in as many ways as possible.

Remember times when you have had any kind of intuitive experience in the past, or felt some kind of invisible guidance. Past experiences can act as reference points for your future.

 In what form did the guidance come? Was it something you heard inside your head? Did it come in the form of a picture? Or did you feel it as a physical feeling inside your body? Or maybe it was a combination of all those? Imagine that you could give your guidance or intuition a shape or form. Based on your past experiences, what would it look, feel, sound like?

 Can you amplify the feeling, picture, or voice of your inner guide? Ask your unconscious whether it can turn up the volume, the contrast, or the sensation of the sound, picture or feeling so that next time it sends a message to you, you receive it with total clarity.

 How much do you trust your intuition? Keep an intuition list to validate the feelings you have that are correct. Write down every time you have an intuition about something. Check back from time to time and notice how often you were correct. Soon you will learn how to distinguish between inner guidance and thought clutter.

 Relax from time to time and practise mind mapping – just putting down whatever freeform creative ideas come into your mind concerning a subject. The more you do this, the more your inner guide will get used to being given permission to come through.

 Thank your inner guide whenever it gives you a message. This reinforces the message to your unconscious that you want to listen to your inner guide. The more you value your inner guide the more messages it will give you. Imagine it is another aspect of your brain and value what it tells you as much as you value your logical or emotional intelligence.

Mike's story:
The case of the perfect landlord

I decided to move to Paris to find work in the media. I took a leap of faith and crated up my belongings, not knowing where I was going to live.

I knew exactly what I wanted; I wrote it down: a one-bedroom flat in the centre of town for the equivalent of less than a thousand pounds a month – maybe a tad optimistic. Oh, and no commission or deposit because I didn't have the cash. I also really wanted the flat to be near greenery and a ten-minute cycle ride from a station. I added to my list a great relationship with my landlord and a place where my neighbours would have no problem with me playing music.

Some friends offered to have me to stay. However, they were concerned that it would take me up to six months to find a good flat in the centre. And they thought I was being totally unrealistic about the rent! We agreed that I would limit my stay to two weeks and then, whatever happened in the meantime, I would move out.

The pressure was really on. I arrived in Paris and moved to my friends' flat with a suitcase full of my belongings.

On the first night, I got a call from a friend in Spain. She said that she could give me one contact – a friend who had a flat in the centre of town, though she didn't know what it was like. I rang the landlord and he said I could come to see it a few days later.

I also rang some estate agents and made appointments to see a few flats. None of them were right, so I was panicking a bit by the time I got to see my friend's contact. But when I walked in, I instantly knew it was the right place. It had everything I had written down on my list. Because the landlord was a friend of a friend, he gave me a special price on the rent – amazingly, exactly what I had visualised – and no commission either because no agent was involved.

What's more, even though I play my music and he lives next door, he's become a good friend who pops round for a beer or a glass of wine and helps me with the odd bit of technical stuff on my computer, which I hate doing!

Visualising your cosmic order

If you can't visualise what you want, the cosmos won't be able to either. Visualisation is easy to learn. Even though you may not have thought about it before, you are creating pictures in your head all the time to create your personal experience of reality. You dream, remember, imagine and daydream, all without effort.

When you daydream about the beautiful person you have just met, or what it would be like to escape from the office to a beach somewhere, or even what you are going to eat for lunch, you are creating a reality in your head through the power of your imagination.

Have you ever imagined your boss telling you off for not delivering a project on time, or an argument with your friend, or being old and alone, or being caught doing something wrong? You are also visualising when you mentally rehearse negative scenarios in advance in your head.

By harnessing the power of your unconscious mind through practising deliberate visualisation, you will not only have success in your cosmic orders but also improve your life on a daily basis by getting into the habit of replacing this type of accidental negative daydreaming with a regular flow of positive images into your unconscious.

Think about the list of cosmic orders that you began to develop in Step 3. Which ones would you like to visualise in more detail?

You can visualise anything:

- An object you want
- Improved performance in sports, or business, or examinations
- A thinner body
- Improved health and healing

Jot down any thoughts you have about what you are currently unable to picture clearly and what you would like to able to visualise in more detail.

What I want to visualise in more detail
●●

_____

_____

_____

_____

_____

_____

_____

_____

_____

Here is a series of exercises to increase your visualisation power. By practising these, you will become more and more proficient at visualising your goals.

Visualising colour

 Sit quietly. Close your eyes. Feel the eyelids relax until the point where the muscles just won't work.

 With your eyes still closed, roll your eyes up inside your head as if you are looking at your eyebrows.

 Now take a deep breath in, hold it for a count of 10 and then let the breath out. Take another breath, hold it for 10 and then exhale. Take a third breath in the same way so that you begin to feel your breath slowing down. As you breathe more and more deeply, you will begin to feel your whole body relaxing as if waves of relaxation are flowing from the top of your head right down to your toes. Relax into your alpha state.

 Now imagine that you are looking at a coloured ball in front of you.

 Now take a paintbrush in your mind and paint the ball a different colour.

 Practise painting the ball all the different colours of the rainbow. Change the ball to red,
then orange,
then yellow,
then green,
then blue,
then indigo,
and finally violet.

Whenever you are ready to finish, say to yourself, 'When I open my eyes, I will be feeling alert and wonderful.' Open your eyes. If you are experienced, you will be able to come fully awake just by opening your eyes. Alternatively, you can follow the instructions for counting upwards from 1 to 5 in your mind on page 125. In either case, make sure that you get up slowly.

Visualising numbers

 Sit quietly. Close your eyes. Feel the eyelids relax until the point where the muscles just won't work.

 With your eyes still closed, roll your eyes up inside your head as if looking at your eyebrows.

 Now take a deep breath in, hold it for a count of 10 and then let the breath out. Take another breath, hold it for 10 and then exhale. Take a third breath in the same way so that you begin to feel your breath slowing down. As you breathe more and more deeply, you will begin to feel your whole body relaxing as if waves of relaxation are flowing from the top of your head right down to your toes.

 Relax into your alpha state.

> Imagine you have a paintbrush or a pen.
> Paint the number 1 in front of you in your mind's eye.
> Now erase it with an imaginary eraser.
> Next paint the number 2 in front of you.
> Now erase it.
> Next paint the number 3 in front of you.

Now erase it.

Continue to paint numbers from 4 to 10.

 Finally, go through the process one more time, painting numbers, but this time imagine that each one is a different colour.

Paint number 1 red,

number 2 orange,

number 3 yellow,

number 4 green,

number 5 blue,

number 6 indigo,

number 7 violet.

 Whenever you are ready to finish, say to yourself, 'When I open my eyes, I will be feeling alert and wonderful.' Open your eyes. If you are experienced, you will be able to come fully awake just by opening your eyes. Alternatively, you can follow the instructions for counting upwards from 1 to 5 in your mind on page 125. In both cases, make sure that you get up slowly.

Visualising shapes

 1 Sit quietly. Close your eyes. Feel the eyelids relax until the point where the muscles just won't work.

 2 With your eyes still closed, roll your eyes up inside your head as if looking at your eyebrows.

 3 Now take a deep breath in, hold it for a count of 10 and then let the breath out. Take another breath, hold it for 10 and then exhale. Take a third breath in the same way so that you begin to feel your breath slowing down. As you breathe more and more deeply, you will begin to feel your whole body relaxing as if waves of relaxation are flowing from the top of your head right down to your toes.

 4 Relax into your alpha state.

> Imagine you have a circle in front of you.
> Colour it in with a colour of your choosing.
> Erase it.
> Imagine you have a square.
> Colour it in with a colour of your choosing.
> Erase it.
> Imagine you have a triangle.
> Colour it in with a colour of your choosing.
> Erase it.
> Imagine you have a three-dimensional box in front of you.
> Colour it in with a colour of your choosing.
> Turn the box around in your mind's eye so that it spins in front of you.

 5 Whenever you are ready to finish, say to yourself, 'When I open my eyes, I will be feeling alert and wonderful.' Open your eyes. If you are experienced, you will be able to come fully awake just by opening your eyes. Alternatively, you can follow the instructions for counting upwards from 1 to 5 in your mind on page 125. In either case, make sure that you get up slowly.

Visualising yourself

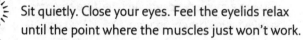

1. Sit quietly. Close your eyes. Feel the eyelids relax until the point where the muscles just won't work.

2. With your eyes still closed, roll your eyes up inside your head as if looking at your eyebrows.

3. Now take a deep breath in, hold it for a count of 10 and then let the breath out. Take another breath, hold it for 10 and then exhale. Take a third breath in the same way so that you begin to feel your breath slowing down. As you breathe more and more deeply, you will begin to feel your whole body relaxing as if waves of relaxation are flowing from the top of your head right down to your toes.

4. In your mind's eye, see your own body standing in front of you as a three-dimensional image.

5. Look at the outside of your body, scanning your body from the front from top to toe. Study your head and face. What do you look like? Look at your torso, your arms, your legs, your hands and your feet.

6. How much detail can you notice? What does your hair look like? Your eyes? Your nose? Your mouth? Your fingernails? The shape of your calves? Your big toe? Your thumb? Your little finger? Do you have any birthmarks? Any wrinkles?

Next, turn your body round and look at your back. How much detail can you notice about yourself from this side? How would you describe what you see?

 Notice your height and weight. Whenever you are ready to finish, say to yourself, 'When I open my eyes, I will be feeling alert and wonderful.' Open your eyes. If you are experienced, you will be able to come fully awake just by opening your eyes. Alternatively, you can follow the instructions for counting upwards from 1 to 5 in your mind on page 125. In either case, make sure that you get up slowly.

Summary Step 5

- Practise entering your alpha state so that you can get in touch with your intuition and inner guidance on a regular basis.
- Acknowledge, when you receive guidance from your inner guide.
- Practise visualisation – the more detailed your visualisation, the more you will amplify the power of the cosmic orders you project to the universe.

Step 6:
Place your order

'By asking for the impossible we obtain the best possible.'

PROVERB

Are you ready?

Now you've completed all the stages needed to create your cosmic order – discovering what you want in each area of your life (see Step 3), getting in touch with your imagination and listening to your higher guidance.

It's time for the final step but one – placing your order. There are four parts to this:

- Preparation
- Visualisation – preparing to place your order
- What I call 'pressing send' – the bit where you actually send your request off
- Saying 'thank you' in advance

Relax, though; this can all be achieved in a matter of minutes once you get used to the process.

1: Preparation

To begin, you are going to draw upon the ability to relax that you developed in Step 5. But this time you are going to build up your energy through rhythmic breathing.

Rhythmic breathing and why you need it

Rhythmic breathing is similar to deep breathing. As you inhale and exhale, you breathe to the same count on the in and out breaths. With practise you can establish a rhythm in tune with your heartbeat. The more you practise the better you get.

You can place an order without rhythmic breathing, but I have found over the last ten years that I have a far higher success rate when I breathe for at least ten minutes or so before placing the order.

There are two reasons for this. Firstly, once you breathe to an even rhythm you quickly go into an alpha trance state. As you know from the previous Step, this is the best state in which to visualise what you want – which ensures that you are transmitting exactly what you want to transmit to the universe.

Of course you could just use all your practise in reaching the alpha state that you gained in the previous Step and go straight to the visualisation stage in this Step and then press enter/send. But there is a second, very important reason to do rhythmic breathing. By breathing before you send off your order, you raise your energy and vibration level and this amplifies the power of your order.

Ancient traditions such as yoga say that when you learn to breathe in a rhythmic fashion, your body is getting used to going back to a natural rhythm: that is, the rhythm and vibration of the cosmos.

As you know, everything in the universe has a vibration and a rhythm – the tides, the molecules and atoms that make up the universe, the movement of the Sun, the Moon and the planets, even the cells of our bodies. Ancient medicine and philosophy recognised this. Now belatedly, science is becoming aware that everything in our universe is not static but moving.

In everyday life, when you are breathing normally your vibration is lower than when you breathe more deeply. This is because deep breathing raises the level of life-force energy both in your physical and non-physical, or auric, bodies. This energy is called Qi (Ch'i) by the Chinese, Prana in Indian philosophy, and Mana by the ancient Hawaiians.

By raising your Qi through control of your breath, you cease to be separate from the rest of the universe. Instead, you can contact that part of the universe outside time and space where the future is formed. Rhythmic breathing raises the level of energy in your system to match the levels of energy in that part of the universe.

You will find that as well as increasing your cosmic ordering effectiveness, there are many other benefits to practising rhythmic breathing regularly. The breath sends more oxygen into your system, so you will feel much more alert and focused. It also releases toxins out of your body.

Building up your energy: rhythmic breathing

In this exercise, the rhythm of breathing is 2, 1, 2, 1 – in other words, you hold your breath for half the time of the inhale and exhale breath, which are the same length.

In the example opposite, I suggest an inhale of 8 counts (seconds) and that you hold your breath for a count of 4. If you find that too long to do initially, you can reduce the length of the breath to an inhale of 4 or 6, hold for 2 or 3, exhale for 4 or 6, hold for 2 or 3. But with time, you will find that you can increase the depth and duration of the breath. As you do this, the build-up of Qi life-force energy in your physical and auric bodies will be increased.

To practise getting really comfortable with the process, you can do this exercise as often as you wish. Before you use rhythmic breathing to precede the sending of an order, I suggest that, at a minimum, you should have already practised for three mornings and evenings for about ten minutes each time.

Sit in a chair. Keep your back straight. You can also sit on the floor, but it is easier to support yourself for a longer period if you are sitting in a chair. Keep your hands separated and resting either on the armrests or in your lap. You can either close your eyes or keep them open – whichever you find most comfortable.

 Breathe in through your nose to the count of 8. As you breathe in, feel the breath filling up your lungs right down to the very bottom. With each breath you are taking in, you are breathing fresh oxygen into your body and also the life-force energy into every pore of your being. You can visualise the breath filling your body with light. As you become practised in deep breathing, you will notice your breath filling up your stomach and then pushing your ribcage sideways so that it expands on the inward breath.

 Hold the breath for four seconds, then exhale for a count of 8. As you exhale, let the breath take any tensions and stresses out of your body. Let the breath leave your body without effort so all the air comes out of your ribcage and stomach.

You don't have to strain in any way to do this. Just gently relax your torso so all the breath is expelled. As the last of the breath is exhaled, your stomach will naturally pull in. Hold your stomach in, empty of air, for four seconds.

 As you practise this breathing regularly, your stomach muscles will strengthen and you will feel more and more comfortable breathing for several minutes. With practice you can increase the time you spend breathing from five to ten minutes and up to half an hour or more.

5 Breathe in groups of four inhales, holds and exhales. This stops you experiencing any discomfort or hyperventilating.

6 Stay in the moment as you breathe. Notice how differently you feel. Say to yourself, *'I am now in service to the universe.'* Ask the universe to send you any thoughts that will help you at this time.

7 Get in touch with the happy, peaceful place inside you on a daily basis.

So remember: After you have practised rhythmic breathing, each time you want to place a cosmic order, breathe for between ten minutes and half an hour to build up your vibration and bring this extra supply of life-force energy into your body. The cosmos will hear your order even more clearly.

In this altered state, you can be 100 per cent present in the moment – the *now* of what you are experiencing. Your attention can focus fully on what you want to experience in the future, so when you see what you want to have in your life, you can fully feel it, see it and hear it as if it is happening to you in the moment.

2: Visualisation – preparing to place your order

After you have raised your energy level, you can place your order. To practise the process, take one of the specific cosmic orders that you have written down. Take a look at it. Is there anything you want to adjust? Or is it ready to go?

Write your order down here:

My cosmic order

....

....

....

....

....

Remember: Look back to the previous steps. Is your order specific and meaningful to you? Is it written down in the present tense and in positive language? Do your beliefs match what you have written? Remember that the universe will give you exactly what you want, whether what you want is conscious or unconscious.

Ecology check on your order

Okay? Now it's time to do an 'ecology' check. What this means is, is your order really going to be good for you when you get it – is it to the good of everyone who may be affected by it?

Really go with your intuition here. Is it 100 per cent good for you? How about your family, or friends, your acquaintances? What about the world at large?

Add on some extras

If you are pretty certain that your order is exactly what you want, but you like double guarantees, how about adding an addendum anyway? I like to say or write down an addition to every order with words that go something like: *'I intend this order be delivered in a way that is good for me and everyone concerned.'*

Or: *'I ask that this order be to the highest good of all concerned.'*

By doing this, you are setting out your intention as clearly as possible for the universe to go ahead and deliver the order.

I also like to add one more statement to every order to allow the universe a bit of space in the co-creation process: *'I ask that the universe deliver this order or whatever is even better than this that will bring the greatest joy into my life.'*

By doing this, I am admitting that I don't know everything. Since the universe is always on my side and acting towards my highest good, why not give it a bit of space and let it bring me the best it can as my partner in creating my future?

Work from the final picture

Now with your written order in front of you, it's time to get your imagination fully activated. You've been practising visualisation in Step 5. It's time to put it to use.

For each cosmic order to be effectively placed, it is important to have a very clear final picture in mind. This final picture represents the last step of your order, or the future piece of evidence that will let you know it has been delivered.

What will have to happen for you to know that your order has been delivered?

This could be a picture of something you see, hear, feel, or say. For example, in the story below, Terri would seem to have been very clear about what she wanted; the order was very specific: an exact sum of money – she even attached a date to it, she even saw the money in her bank account. However, she didn't specify where the money was going to come from, so the universe fulfilled her order in the easiest and quickest way possible that fitted with her belief system.

Terri's story:
The case of the devil in the details

In June I asked the universe for £15,000 to arrive in July. I was very careful to make sure that I didn't ask for it to be earned income as I couldn't see any way to earn that money and for it to be enjoyable at the same time. I was very adamant that the money should come from an unearned source such as a gift. That way, my work/life balance wouldn't suffer. Of course, I was hoping for a lottery win. However, alert to the way the universe can manifest, I was also very conscious to ask that this money come in an ethical way that excluded crime, or a close relative dying and leaving me an inheritance, for example.

I visualised the money coming into my bank account. I thanked the universe for it already having happened. I then forgot about my wish.

In July, my financial advisor rang me for a review. He told me to make some changes to my investments. One of the changes he suggested was to cash in a ten-year-old endowment policy. Remarkably, an organisation was willing to buy it from me, albeit at a fraction of what I had anticipated would have been its maturity value ten years later, but for what he called 'a reasonable amount'. I told him to get on with it. I couldn't be bothered with the details. I knew there was no point in hanging on to the policy. The endowment market had gone down a lot and I knew the policy would never make its anticipated maturity amount. Anything would be good now and it was a bonus that anyone wanted to buy such a policy.

A week later £15,000 arrived in my bank account. I had produced my own unearned income – a gift, but from me to me...

Now, thinking back, I know exactly why it turned out this way. I didn't really believe that I would win the lottery or anything and I didn't want something horrible happening like someone dying and leaving me a legacy. And, I only gave the universe a month, so it didn't have a lot of leeway. The way it turned out, it probably was the best way to get money to me quickly, and the strange thing is, it did feel like a present even though it was my money.

Remember: The universe is a perfect ordering mechanism. It will:

- Always do things in a believable way
- Produce your order in the simplest, most efficient manner possible
- Be 100 per cent accurate and match your order according to the picture(s) you transmit and the amount of emotion attached to the picture

What's your final evidence?

Here's another example. Suppose that your order was that you wanted to get happily married. If you could choose one picture and one piece of evidence for the future that would let you know that you were happily married, what would it be?

Would it be the moment that your spouse placed the ring on your finger? The point on the honeymoon when you realised that you had been married for over a day? Would it be on your fifth wedding anniversary, sitting with your husband or wife and looking back on the good times? Or on your 25th wedding anniversary?

There is no right or wrong answer – it is entirely personal to you. The question is, what will convince you that you have got what you wanted?

What if your cosmic order was for a new home? Would your final picture be of the moment you placed the key in the lock and walked into your new home, knowing it belonged to you? Or how about the moment you put your signature on the contract? Or perhaps it would be a picture of you sitting in your new home having a cup of tea.

To practise this, take the order you wrote down on the worksheet above. Now write down your final picture in as much detail as possible.

You can copy this worksheet as many times as you like, so that you can use it with each cosmic order that you send.

Flo's story:
The case of the arms that held me

I visualised sitting on a beach with my ideal man's arms wrapped around me. Music was playing in the background – just like in a film – the soundtrack to my life, as we watched a sunset together. At the time I visualised this, I was as far away as possible from a beach – in the middle of London with no prospect of a holiday.

A year later I found myself in California at the beach with a new man. As the sun set, I felt his arms wrapped around me and I suddenly remembered the picture. Then I heard the jazz playing nearby. We went out together for a year afterwards.

Creating a final picture of your cosmic order

Cosmic order from page 147	Final picture/piece of evidence that will let me know I have got my order

Now take a look at what you have written. Are you happy with it?

Changing your cosmic order into a future memory

For the universe to fulfil your order, you need to make your picture of the future as real as your picture would be of a past memory. In fact, we call this 'creating a future memory'.

How do you create a future memory? By trying your final picture on for size and adding in a strong positive feeling.

 Look at the final picture you have written down.

 Next, relax. If you are doing this as a seamless process, you will already be in your alpha state because you will have relaxed through rhythmic breathing. However, if this is your first practice, for now just go back to the alpha level of relaxation in the way you have got used to for the visualisation exercises in Step 5.

 When you truly experience an event, it is as if you are living it in the moment. This is called 'being associated'. When you are 'associated' you feel it as if it is happening to you right now and you become absorbed into the experience. If you want a reference point for this, imagine something enjoyable that has happened to you in the past. Immediately, you can probably step into that experience as if it is actually happening to you right now: you can see what is happening around you, through your own eyes, and you can probably easily experience the pleasant feelings that you had at the time.

 Now you are going to do the same for your cosmic order final picture and, by doing so, you will make this imagined future event into a reality.

Tip **The universe is perfect**

Your unconscious believes emotion more than words. If you just express an order in words, the universe won't take any notice. But when you try the picture on, and experience it in the moment as if it is happening to you right now, your picture becomes a memory in your future. Your unconscious and the universe make no distinction between something that 'really' has happened to you and the memory you have put into your future. Both of them are as real as each other. And because there is no time and space in the non-physical part of the universe, it doesn't matter that your 'real' memory is in the past, and your final cosmic order picture is in the future. In cosmic terms, they both exist in a place where there is no past or future and so both are equally 'real'.

 Step into the picture as if it is an experience happening to you right now, so that you can see what is going on through your own eyes. Look around. What are you feeling? What are you seeing? What are you saying to yourself? What are you hearing? What other sounds are there in the experience? What are you touching? What emotions are going on in your body? Remember the more positive you feel in this present experience, the more positive the feeling will be with the delivery of your order. You are creating the reality in your future with the reality you are constructing in this present moment. Let yourself go in the flow of the experience.

 While you are there, double check – it's always worth it. Is this the best final picture that you can create?

 Great. Now step out of your picture and this time see exactly the same experience happening to you, but as if it is a film with you as the main player. So, unlike the previous step where you were actually experiencing the scene as if it was happening to you in the present moment, this time you can see your body in the picture.

This is called dissociation. Dissociation means that you are the observer of an experience; in other words, you are thinking about it rather than actually being in it. Instead of seeing the experience through your own eyes and feeling all the senses of that experience as if it is happening now, you see a picture of the experience with *you* in it – as if it is a film or a story rather than a sensory experience that your body is part of.

 To place a cosmic order, it is always essential *both* to have imagined what it is like to really live the experience in advance and also to see it happening to you as a dissociated experience. The reason is that dissociating as a final step in the process is rather like putting a big cross in the line going from your present to your future. The unconscious stores dissociated events as future events. It says to your unconscious something along the lines of: 'Although I know now that this will happen because I know what it feels like to have it in my life, I am making a distinction between my past memories and this as a future memory.'

Remember:

When you are 'associated':

- You feel, see and hear the experience through your senses as if it is happening right now
- You experience it 'through your own eyes'
- This registers the experience as a memory in your unconscious

When you are 'dissociated':

- You are 'aware of' the experience, but are not 'in' the experience
- You can see your body in the picture as if it is a story or film happening to you
- You are an observer of the event
- This registers in your unconscious as a memory, but distinguishes it as a future memory rather than a past memory

Dody's story:
The case of the missing picture

Every summer I run a residential art course for talented children. Because they are not earning, I try to find ways for the children to have the cost of the course subsidised. But even though I am putting myself out for them, they don't for me. I always have to pursue them at the last minute to find out whether they are definitely coming on the course.

This year I decided to use cosmic ordering to make sure my course ran smoothly. I wrote out my order: 'I intend to attract ten groups of children for the course.' I saw a picture of the children ringing me up and asking to come on the course.

The course was in July. I needed to know numbers by the end of June. I had had enquiries from more than ten groups, but only seven had signed up. Why wasn't my order working?

Then I suddenly realised. I looked at the wording of my order. Of course, I had only asked that I attract ten groups. My picture was wrong. I had totally forgotten to ask that the ten groups also sign up and pay. I changed my order and my picture, and by the end of the week the course was full!

3: Pressing 'send'

Once you have placed, or prepared, your order, that's it. Now your order is ready to go. Your finger is poised over the 'enter' button on the computer.

How exactly do you send the order?

Here's the great secret. There is no 'send' button! Or, you could say there are a thousand ways to press 'send' and all of them are right. That's not a cop-out. It really is true. You see, once you have done all the preparation, what really counts is your intention and belief that your order will come true. By this time you should feel totally confident about your order. You've already experienced it. Your unconscious is already transmitting it as a future memory. You've filled the memory with life-force energy through your breathing.

But, your unconscious does appreciate ritual and closure, so here are some ways you may want to finish off the process – just so you feel that you have pressed a 'send' button after you have completed the *Changing your cosmic order into a future memory* section.

Choose whichever way feels comfortable and fits with your belief system.

Six ways to press the 'send' button

Here are a few of the many ways to press 'send'. Add your own to the list.

State your intention verbally: As you complete the process, express your intention aloud: *'I intend that this cosmic order is now realised in the most positive way possible.'*

Or: *'My intention is that this be manifested in my life in the most positive way possible.'*

See your cosmic order in your future: Visualise yourself putting your cosmic order into your future, just as if you could reach your hand in, open it up and let the picture of your future slide effortlessly into place amongst all the other events in your past, present and future.

Post your cosmic order: Burn the piece of paper on which you have written your order (preferably first take it out of this book!). Obviously, be careful how you do this. Make sure that you watch the paper as it burns and make sure that you burn it in a vessel that doesn't overheat and set any neighbouring objects on fire. As the order burns and turns to flame and smoke, see it being delivered in the smoke and ashes to the universe to take care of. If you like, imagine asking your guardian angel to deliver it for you. Or simply see in your mind the order popping through a cosmic postbox, or through the cosmic internet, being registered in the cosmic storehouse.

Place your order on an altar: Many people like to have a special place in their home that acts as a sacred space or altar. You can put all your cosmic orders on your altar and, as you do this, light a candle, or make a wish, asking that your orders be manifested.

If you would like to have an altar, it is easy to make one. Simply choose a small corner anywhere in your home. It doesn't have to be very big, just somewhere that you can set aside and keep clear for objects that have a special meaning for you. For example, you can put your dream box here and any other objects such as candles, crystals, pictures of angels, saints or guides, or any other religious or mystical symbols, depending on your belief system. To add extra energy into your cosmic orders, bless the space by imagining that it is surrounded with white light. Each day, infuse the space with energy by visualising white light around it. You can also hold your left hand above the space with the palm facing upwards and visualise energy coming in from above, and hold your right hand above your altar with the palm facing downwards and visualise the energy flowing outwards through your palm into the altar and your cosmic orders.

To intensify the energy, you can place your altar within a bigger sacred space in the home. To do this, set aside a bigger corner of a room, or indeed a whole room if you have the space, and use this space solely for your daily alpha meditation and rhythmic breathing work. This will raise the Qi vibration of the space in which your orders are, so that they are permanently surrounded by positive feelings.

Walk out your future: Depending on the space you need, you can do this either in a room or outside. Imagine that there is a line going from your present to your future. You will have an intuitive sense of which direction your past, present and future is in. Turn and face your future so that it is in front of you. Your timeline may only be a few paces long, or it may run over several hundred metres. Take as much space as you need. It can be incredibly liberating to see your future out in front of you.

Start walking along the line into your future. When you get

to the date of your order, stop there for a moment and visualise yourself firmly planting the final-picture future memory in this place. If you have several cosmic orders, you can plant one after another wherever they belong in your future path.

After you have completed the process, either walk back along your timeline to where you started – the present – or if you like, you can sneak a peak at how your future has changed now that your orders are in place. Simply carry on walking along the path to your future. If your intuition tells you to stop, do so. Stand for a moment and ask your unconscious, *'Where in the future am I?'* A date will come to mind. Next ask yourself, *'What's going on here?'* See what answer comes to mind. Notice what you feel, too. Do any images come to mind? Any thoughts, any emotions, any general impressions? Just quietly register what happens, and ask yourself, *'How does this relate to my cosmic order?'* Sometimes you will get an answer that will give you an insight into your life, or guidance for other orders you might want to place. After you have finished this process, return to *now* by walking back to where you started.

Dream delivery: You can also post your order just before you go to bed. Sit up in bed and do your rhythmic breathing. Lie down to visualise the final picture process so that you are relaxed. As the final piece of the process, visualise the picture of you dissociated in your film being lifted up into the air above your head and posted into a postbox marked 'Cosmic request box'. As you do this, know that as you fall asleep and begin to dream, your guardian angel, or the universe, will come to empty out the request box, collect your cosmic order and begin to process it.

FAQs

Is there a difference between 'placing' and 'sending' an order? Do I have to 'press send' for my order to be realised?

'Placing the order' is used here as a description for the whole process of thinking through your order and sending it. In reality, as soon as you have thought through your order in the ways described above and fully intend that it will be realised, the universe hears your thoughts as the order. But using a ritual to 'send your order' in addition is useful, since it acts as a convincer for your conscious mind that you have actually taken an action towards your order. This helps to maintain your 100 per cent belief in the order delivery – an essential ingredient in its success.

Do I need to place my order more than once?

No, absolutely not. Once you have used whatever ritual you choose to place an order, know that the order has been received and is in the process of being delivered. To let go of attachment, it is a good idea either to burn the paper you have written your order on, or to put it away and not look at the order again until the point at which you think it has been delivered.

4: Saying thank you in advance

Whichever way you choose to place your order, *always* say to the universe: '*Thank you in advance for delivering my order.*'

This once again confirms to the universe that you absolutely believe that the order already exists and is waiting to be delivered at the appropriate time.

If you say this rather than something along the lines of, '*Please deliver my order,*' by using *please* instead of *thank you*, you are automatically suggesting that there is some doubt as to whether or not the universe will deliver. As soon as you do that, the universe will sense your uncertainty and your order will not be as successful.

So, be focused, firm and grateful.

FAQs

Can I make an order on behalf of someone else?
You can't live someone else's life for them. Each of us has free will and choice to create our own reality. But the idea that we are all separate from each other is a myth: we are all joined together in the non-physical part of the universe. Have you ever heard of a group mind? Groups of people can create a joint reality through shared belief systems – that's why some families or even whole countries keep repeating patterns of circumstances and

events. Their expectations cause the circumstances to recur. So what each of us thinks influences the other. It's been shown that if a teacher believes that a student will do well, they actually will do better. Make sure you always hold a positive mental picture of the people around you.

Can I place an order for something small, for example somewhere to park when I get home late in the evening?

Yes, the universe is a vast, abundant and non-judgemental storehouse for any order that will make your life better and easier as long as you are not doing harm to anyone in the process.

If you want to make sure that you can park easily, or that your car or house is protected from break-ins, or that you are always free from traffic hold-ups, place a cosmic order and visualise it. For example, as you drive home, see yourself parking in your wide parking space. Or before you set out in the morning, visualise clear roads. Before you come back home, visualise your house waiting for you all safe, secure and welcoming.

If you are ever stuck in traffic, see the traffic flowing again, and your car moving smoothly down the road again. Within a short time, you should find the flow of the traffic is restored.

The possibilities are endless. The only limits are those within your imagination.

Summary Step 6

- First check your order: check that it meets all the rules of cosmic ordering – that it's specific, is in the present tense, positively expressed, and personal to you.

- Check the 'ecology' of the order.

- What is your final picture – the future piece of evidence that will let you know when your order has been delivered?

- Build up your energy through breathing. This increases your life force and raises the frequency of your vibration to match that of the cosmos. It takes you into an alpha trance state.

- Create a future memory. Now step into your order and visualise it. Experience it 'associated', as if it is happening right now.

- Next, step out of your order and experience it 'dissociated' – see it like a film in which you are the main character.

- Press 'send'.

- Say thank you because the universe is in the process of delivering your order right now.

Step 7:

Let the universe decide the how

'Energy is eternal delight.'

WILLIAM BLAKE

Believe then see

When you buy something in a shop you know that your credit card payment has been accepted once you have got a receipt. With the cosmos, though, we have to provide our own receipts for our orders – the universe isn't going to send you proof that your order is on its way the minute you press the 'send' button. When you place a cosmic order, you have to believe then see, not see then believe.

The only way for your order to be delivered to you is to trust absolutely that as soon as – the minute and second – you have gone through the visualisation process for your final picture, and set your intention with the cosmos, your order has been instantly received and is already in the process of being delivered. A cosmic order only works if you let go of *all* attachment to it.

Trust and let go

What does that actually mean? That you fully trust, believe and allow the universe to deliver your order.

Yes, *it is okay* to allow yourself to notice signs that you are on track to get what you have asked for.

Yes, you *can* take actions towards what you want. In fact, taking action is a sign that you fully believe that you will get what you have asked for. It's a commitment by you to the universe, choosing to give time to gaining what you want. The universe will, in return, throw you the odd synchronicity to say *'Your order's on its way.'* More on that in a moment.

But, here's the paradox. Don't go *searching* for signs – and certainly not *obsessively* – that your order is on its way. As soon as you start doing this, what you are really saying to the universe is: 'I don't trust you. Give me some proof that I'm on track.' The only reason you would have to do that would be if you either wanted your order too much, or you wanted to control how the universe delivers the order to you. Neither is a good idea.

Keep the oven door shut

You know what happens if you keep opening the oven door to see if the cake is ready? The cake doesn't cook faster. It may even collapse in the middle. Yes, you do have a big role in the making of the cake – you decide the recipe, you gather the ingredients together, you mix them all up, you decide the temperature of the oven, the time the cake should be ready. *But* the cake can't cook faster than it cooks. It doesn't matter whether you check it again and again. It won't be ready any faster.

Just as you can ruin a cake by worrying too much about when it's going to be ready, you can ruin your order by worrying too much about the timing.

Here's another analogy: when you plant a seed in the ground, what would happen if you kept digging it up to check on its progress? It would probably die. You have to trust that eventually it will break through the earth to reach the sunlight and turn into a seedling and eventually a beautiful flower.

> *When you place a cosmic order, you will have to operate in the dark for a while.*

FAQs

Why do orders sometimes happen only when I have forgotten about them?

This is down to your detachment. Here's an example: a couple are desperate to have a baby, but after being told they cannot, eventually give up and adopt, only to find later the wife becomes pregnant. How does this work? This is entirely down to over-attachment. In this case the couple desperately wanted their own baby but the key word is 'desperately' – they were over-attached. When their attention was on the adopted baby, they let go of the over-attachment (but not desire) for their own baby and this allowed the universe to deliver the original order.

Can I ask for something to come at a specific time and still let go of attachment to it?

It's perfectly fine to ask for what you want at a specific time. You can be so specific that you can ask for something in one hour's time and the universe can deliver it. There is no time and space in the non-physical part of the universe, so it doesn't matter to the cosmos whether you ask for something in three years' time or in one day's time. However, you may believe that you have more control over the near than the distant future. So many people find it easier to let go of attachment to orders far ahead in the future because they know they can't control events in the long term with willpower.

The universe knows how better than you do

Letting go of attachment also means that you let go of the way the universe will deliver your order. It will deliver your order in the way that it can best find to do it.

Your role in the creation process is to decide the *what*. The role of the universe is to decide the *how*.

Vincent's story:
The case of the universe knowing best

I always wanted to be a storyteller. I decided to give up my highly paid job as a business trainer. For two years I lived off my savings and wrote a novel. I saw myself as the next John Grisham, writing bestsellers. I had always loved telling stories, ever since I was a child. I didn't really care what kind of book I wrote, but since my savings would run out at some time and I had a mortgage to pay and responsibility to my wife and two daughters to earn some money, I thought I had better concentrate on a relatively commercial area of writing. In fact, I only meant to write for one year, but at the end of the first year I hadn't achieved what I wanted and so my wife agreed to keep on working. I could carry on writing and look after the children. Nearly two years in, money was getting tight. But just before my self-imposed deadline, I finished my book. I sent it to agents all over the UK. I had a few letters back. Most of them didn't even bother to reply, but I expected that. I was still undaunted and convinced something would happen very soon. After all, I knew I was a storyteller.

Some time later, still nothing and money was really running short now. My wife, who had believed in me so strongly, was pregnant again. One evening we had a heated discussion and she insisted that I would have to at least look for some part-time work. Coincidentally, a few days later I bumped into an ex-colleague in the supermarket. He too had given up work, but was training in a new company. He told me that the new company used part-time and self-employed trainers. He gave me a contact and a telephone number.

I started working for the company from time to time, and after a while was designing training sessions. Only two months after I had started, the head of training came to me and asked me to design a new training course – telling stories as a way of showing people in the company how to pass on skills and knowledge to others. Of course I leapt at the chance. And now I do it in other companies, too. I knew I was a storyteller. I don't care about the book any more. This is much more me. It turns out I was right, but somebody out there knew better than me how best to apply my talent!

Have patience – you can't always make sense of things until the end

Have you ever started a jigsaw puzzle? Nowadays you can get a whole variety of jigsaws, from simple pictures to really elaborate ones with huge amounts of detail. You know what it is like when you first see the picture on the box. But once you start the jigsaw there's always a point with even the simplest one when it looks impossible to complete. You can probably remember sitting with the picture in front of you, knowing exactly what you are supposed to end up with, but with hundreds of tiny, odd-shaped pieces of jigsaw in front of you – bits of colour here and there that look like they might or might not relate to the final picture. Right at the beginning, they don't always look as if they are going to slot together easily, or make sense at all, or ever make up the end picture. Even though you have the picture on the box to act as a guide, it is daunting at the outset because you don't know how easy the puzzle will be to complete.

Generally, you start just by looking for any piece that fits the picture. Then, once you have found one, you find another, possibly two or three more pieces that start to fit together. Gradually, using the picture on the box as your guide, you begin to see patterns in the pieces of puzzle in front of you. As you keep looking for more pieces where the shape or colour fit together, eventually there comes a point where suddenly you realise you can see that the picture has started to come through and it is absolutely clear that you are on track.

Your final picture is already out there. You haven't found all the pieces of jigsaw that will lead you to it, but the moment you sent your order, the first piece was in place and the picture was on the box. Piece by piece, even when you don't think you are getting anywhere, the universe will be putting the pieces together that will keep you on track. Your part is just to remember from time to time where you are heading – that final picture you put into your future.

> **Remember:** The universe knows where you are and how to find you. It doesn't matter whether you are at a party, walking down the street, sitting at home or trekking in Peru. If you are due an order, the delivery service will search you out and get it to you somehow.

Take action to keep focus

The rabbit and the stump

Once upon a time there was a hard-working farmer living in a poor part of the countryside. It was hard even to earn enough money to buy food. In the middle of one of his fields there was a stump where a tree had once stood.

One day a fat rabbit ran into the stump in the middle of the night. The impact broke its neck and it died. When the farmer walked through his field the following morning, he found the dead rabbit and was very excited at his good fortune. He decided that not only had his luck changed, but he would also clearly never have to work again. He threw away all his farm implements and his plough and sat guarding the tree stump night and day waiting for another fat rabbit to break its neck on it. But, of course, day after day, night after night, nothing happened. No rabbit appeared and the farmer became the laughing stock of the countryside.

TRADITIONAL STORY

Knowing that the universe will find you no matter what doesn't mean you should just sit there. *You* can *and* should *take action towards achieving what you want.*

As the Bible says, 'God helps those who help themselves.' Taking action shows your belief in your eventual success. If you take no action, as in the story above, the universe won't believe that you are committed to your order.

How the universe delivers

But, here's another paradox: your actions may not lead to the result in the *way* you expect.

Taking action towards achieving what you want shows *focus* – by taking action, you convince the universe that you really are firmly convinced that your cosmic order will be delivered, so it does deliver it.

The universe will still deliver your order to you in the *way* it thinks is best, however.

How to take action

How, then, should you take action? What kind of actions should you take?

Firstly, take any step that you think is in the direction of your order, even if it doesn't pay dividends immediately. For example, if you want a new relationship, start going to places where you will meet lots of people, join a dating agency, or take a dance class. It doesn't matter if you think that you won't meet the right type of people there – you are still showing commitment.

Secondly, when you take action, take action softly. The Chinese Taoist philosopher Lao Tse put this nicely. He noticed that gentleness and softness always overcome hardness and toughness. He said the teeth are one of the toughest parts of the body, but they often fall out before you get old, while the tongue is one of the softest parts, but it lasts until you die. In the same way, in nature a tree stands tall and strong, but can be toppled by a wind. However, water, which is soft, can wear away the hardest stone eventually.

> *You don't have to be tough, you don't have to be firm, you don't need to use willpower, you don't need to struggle to get what you want in life. You only need focus and belief.*

The how is always an effortless process. Just keep your focus and stay in the flow of what you want. After you have sent your order off, simply keep your focus on what you want, take action in the direction of what you want and, at the same time, forget about what you want. Stay in the flow.

The analogy that is often used to describe this process is that of a boat being rowed down a river. Point the bow of the boat in the direction in which you want to head. Keep rowing while you enjoy the scenery around you. Tune into the flow of the river as you row. You don't have to push against the river current. You simply allow the boat to take you at a natural pace around each bend, seeing the beautiful scenery that will greet you.

In other words, do everything to keep yourself heading in the direction of what you want, and you will attract the right people and circumstances to you. Simply trust that the universe will deliver the *how*.

Trust and everything will fall in your favour because you are in tune with the unfolding process of life.

Be open to clues from the universe

When you ask for something a long time in the future, how do you sustain your faith and belief over that period of time?

The universe does give us some clues that our orders are in the post. These clues are known as *synchronicities*.

A synchronicity is a seeming coincidence or happenstance. Sometimes a synchronicity is preceded by a gut feeling, dream or intuition. Perhaps your order is to have a change of career. Suddenly you catch sight of an advertisement that says: 'Are you ready for a career change?'

Or perhaps you want a long-term romantic relationship. You have modelled the person you want on a famous film star. Suddenly, every magazine you open has pictures of that particular film star in it.

Maybe you want to check that you really do believe it is possible to have a happy relationship because that's what you have asked for. You walk into a restaurant and catch sight of a couple on the table next to you. Suddenly, the man gets down on one knee and you hear and see him proposing to his girlfriend.

Or you have a picture of your ideal car – only available by import to the country. One day you take a wrong turning, walk round the corner and there is a car exactly like the one you want.

When the universe throws you signals like this, it is showing you that you are right to keep your faith. It is saying, 'Just hang on a little bit longer! The forces of the universe are lined up on your side.'

FAQs

What kind of choice or opportunity is synchronicity?
It is the job offer out of the blue that doesn't necessarily look the logical choice, but taking it leads you to the eventual career opportunity you always wanted. It is the seemingly boring invitation that leads you into the bar where you meet the perfect partner. Or it is the traffic delay that causes you to take a different road where you see your perfect home for sale, even though you don't necessarily realise it is your perfect home until much later.

Synchronicity is the luck that can happen whenever you give it a chance to show itself. It can bring about a dramatic change in your circumstances, or your understanding of yourself and your life.

How will I know when this is an opportunity I should take?
The only clue to this type of opportunity is the gut instinct you have when it happens. Follow this instinct and you can't go wrong.

A choice and an opportunity

Often a synchronicity is an opportunity for you to make a choice. A synchronicity may precede a sudden change in our circumstances or herald an opportunity that, if we take it, will direct us to the event or place where our order is waiting to be delivered to us.

The Eureka moment

Sometimes the synchronicity is the thought itself, the one that leaps into your head, seemingly out of the blue – the Eureka moment that precedes a huge leap forward in your thinking and clears the path to your dream. One famous example of synchronicity is Albert Einstein. In 1907 he was suddenly struck by the thought: 'A person freely falling has no weight', and soon afterwards he followed up with his new theory of gravitation in his General Theory of Relativity.

Dianne's story:
The case of the unexpected boyfriend

I asked the cosmos for a new boyfriend. Because I didn't want to get over-attached as to how he came into my life, I asked that he appear in the most unexpected way possible. But, because I was keen to get things moving, I put a date on the time of his arrival – November. I would be going on a business trip for almost the whole of that month and travelling to all sorts of interesting places in America and Europe. I figured that if a boyfriend was going to come into my life in the most unexpected way, he was likely to come in one of the places where I was meeting new people in situations I had never been in before.

I bought myself a new wardrobe and had my hair done and went off on my travels. In three weeks I met no one. I came back home and thought, 'That didn't work.' I had been out, I had made sure I had hung around the best places and still no one had appeared.

A couple of days after I came home, I went to see some friends for Sunday brunch. Since they lived in a very laid-back part of town, it didn't seem worth making a big effort, so I hadn't washed my hair, I was wearing a dreadful old pair of jogging trousers and a very scraggy T-shirt. My friend Jill and I made the food while her husband was outside fixing the car, which was having engine problems. When the food was ready, Jill called him in. The husband didn't appear, the food was getting cold and Jill was getting angry at having her brunch spoiled. Finally, her husband came in with an extra person, a friend of his, who it seemed had turned up to help him.

Because the atmosphere wasn't very good, I just busied myself with the food and didn't pay the friend much attention. In fact, I have no memory of even noticing what he looked like. We went to sit down on the two sofas after brunch and watch sport on TV. I still hadn't said a word to this guy. He sat next to me and we chatted a bit, but I still hadn't really paid him much attention.

Then, the afternoon over, he offered me a lift home. All fine.

He stopped at my house and kissed me on the cheek goodbye. Then, as I reached towards the door, he leaned over to me and said, 'Can I see you again?'

A few days later we went on our first date. Then we

went on many more. It was only a few weeks later that I realised my new boyfriend had appeared in November, one of the very last days in November, in fact, and certainly in the most unexpected way. Because, of course, I really had expected him to appear overseas and I certainly didn't expect to meet anyone new through my friends – I thought I had met all their friends years ago.

Keep what you have asked for secret

After you have placed your order it helps to keep it secret.

Why? Well, first of all, what you ask for is your business and yours alone.

Second, what normally happens when you tell people about your plans? Maybe some people will be supportive. Some people will say that you are overambitious. Others may think that you are being fantastical. Friends or family may give you advice – perhaps about being 'realistic', or they may tell you to be 'practical'. Perhaps one or two may sit down and ask how they can help you get what you want.

The trouble is that as soon as you start telling people what you want, your picture may well be clouded by their beliefs and opinions. The clear energy and focus you have directed towards your final picture may become distorted.

What, too, if you have asked for something really big? Will your friends believe that you can and should have something as big as that? Might they be a tiny bit jealous? Or just want to protect you from your own false daydreams?

Even when everyone around you is on your side and eager for you to have your new car, your new career, or your sporting success, what can they really add to your getting it? After all, if you believe 100 per cent that the universe will deliver your order, you don't need their belief to bolster your own. But you certainly don't need their disbelief either.

Tip Ordering relationships

If you visualise a person you would like to have a romantic relationship with, and your future partner is modelled on someone you know, always make sure that you fuzz the features in the face in your picture. For example, it's not going to work if you have a picture of you with Tom Cruise, because Tom Cruise may be putting in entirely different cosmic orders for someone who is nothing like you. However, it is quite okay to say, '*I am with a partner who looks like Tom Cruise*' or '*has all the best qualities that I perceive Tom Cruise to have*'.

Carla's story:
The case of the time-delayed boyfriend
I was living in France for a year and had fallen in love. (Well, now I realise I was more obsessed than anything else.) I had met a guy who was living in Germany but working for the same company as me. Roy seemed to be everything I wanted – he looked great, he was funny and

he was clever. The only thing was that just after I met him I found out that he had a girlfriend. I wasn't interested in seeing someone who wasn't available, so I asked him if he was going to carry on with his relationship. He told me that it was basically over.

I wasn't 100 per cent confident that their relationship really was over. I had been hurt by men in the past. So I decided to ask the universe to deliver a relationship for me.

I visualised a man like Roy in a relationship with me. I knew it would not be okay with the universe to ask for Roy specifically, as you can't make someone fall for you. But I wrote down on a piece of paper that I was now going out with a man with all the qualities Roy had. A man who was available to me. The piece of evidence that would let me know that I had got my dream would be the man like Roy holding me in his arms and saying, 'You don't have to worry. I will take care of you.' Although the first picture that came into my mind was Roy holding me, I deliberately visualised fuzzing out his head in the picture so that I wasn't over-attached to it being Roy, but being a man like Roy (though what I was really thinking was, 'I want it to be Roy').

Nothing happened for a year. I talked to Roy almost every day on the phone. I had lots of work excuses to call him. When I did see him, it felt wonderful but I knew he was still seeing his girlfriend. I kept wondering why the universe wasn't delivering Roy to me. After all, he was my perfect man. I started seeing a counsellor and she told me to let him go, but I couldn't. Then I took a three-week holiday. While I was on holiday I realised I had to do something about this obsession. I decided to apply for another job back in the UK – I was feeling burnt out. I would take a financial risk and retrain as a yoga instructor. Two months later I left my company. Roy said he would be in touch, but I knew he wouldn't.

I went on a yoga training holiday in the sun for a couple of weeks after my job finished. One night I stayed up late with the instructor and a group of the other students in the hotel. Then the other students left and it was just the instructor and me by ourselves. He suddenly gave me a hug. Then he kissed me. We talked for two hours. I told him that I was worried I would have no financial security in my new career. He suddenly put his arms around me and just said, 'You don't have to worry. I will take care of you.' We moved in together two months later.

Now I look back I realise that my order couldn't be delivered until I had let go of the idea that the perfect man I had visualised had to be Roy. And yes, Stefan does have all the qualities I thought Roy had. It turned out that Roy didn't really have them anyway. I had just projected them onto him. In fact, he was having affairs with at least two other girls behind his girlfriend's back. The universe knew better than I did what was right for me.

How to sustain your focus over a long time

Orders may be delivered in days, or you may have to sustain your focus over a much longer time.

Using symbols and energy words are powerful ways of keeping your energy and focus fixed on the final picture of what you want while still letting go of your attachment.

Energy words

An energy word is a word you pick to symbolise the idea of what you want your cosmic order to bring into your life. It is a single word that you can repeat as many times as you like. Like a mantra used in yoga, an energy word calms down the conscious mind and clears a path to the unconscious.

When you learn how to fire walk, you choose a word to say to yourself as you walk across the burning coals. Repeating the word allows you to take your mind away from any thoughts of burning yourself as you walk down the line of hot coals; instead, you simply see the final picture of having reached the end successfully. Your conscious mind is so occupied by the energy word, it can't focus on all the doubts and fears it might otherwise have, but just focuses on its goal.

To demonstrate how powerful an energy word can be, ask a friend to say the word 'no' as you press on his or her outstretched arm. Now ask them to say 'yes'. You should notice that their arm is much stronger when they use a positive rather than a negative word.

How to create an energy word

For any future situation where you want to feel more positive:

 Feel what you want to feel *as if* it is *now*. For example, if you wanted to create a successful presentation or interview, you might want to feel confident or relaxed.

 Choose a word that represents the energy you want to bring into your life. For example, Powerful, Fluent, Confident, Relaxed.

 As you feel what you feel and visualise the energy word, press your thumb and index finger together and say the word three times. This will impress the word and associated feeling into your unconscious.

 The next time you recall the word, press your finger and thumb together at the same time and you will bring back the positive feeling.

Symbols

A symbol is a picture or representation of what you want. You can use your dream picture and dream box (see Step 2) as places to put pictures and symbols to inspire you and keep you motivated. You can also use visualisation of a single picture to create a general feeling of what you want to come into your life. For example, suppose that you have placed an order for a romantic relationship, at the same time you can build up a general feeling of having a romantic relationship by focusing on a single symbol to represent the future relationship. You will still be able to let go of attachment to your order simply because a symbol is so vague and general.

Creating money

Here's a general picture for creating money in your life. Whatever orders you have already placed in relationship to money, you can supplement them with this or a similar visualisation of your choosing.

 1. Close your eyes and imagine that there is a table in front of you. Half of the table is covered with gold and jewels. The other half of the table is piled high with bank notes. Look closely at the bank notes and you will see that they are the highest denomination of bank note possible. There are so many of them that you can't even count them.

 2. As you look at this picture, make sure that you get the feeling of what it is like to be rich.

 3. To bring back this picture to your unconscious mind at any time, choose an energy word to associate with the picture. Any time you want to get back the feeling of wealth, repeat the word. For example, Prosperity, Wealth, Abundance.

Creating a romantic relationship

What symbol would work for you if you want a romantic relationship? Or even a soul mate! A heart is an obvious symbol that works for many people. You can buy a glass heart, or cut a heart out of paper and colour it red. Chose an energy word to associate with this heart. You can, of course, simply use the word 'heart'.

 1. Imagine that you and your dream lover are joined by cords linking heart to heart. Each night before you go to sleep, see your future lover standing in front of you.

2 Notice how the cords joining you are filled with living white energy. Feel his/her presence. Feel how good it is to be in love with each other.

 3 Choose an energy word to bring back this feeling at any time. What word would work for you? Joy, Happiness, Love, Bliss?

 4 What if you want not only a romantic relationship but marriage as well? One symbol that works for many people is the wedding ring itself. To make the feeling of being married as real as possible, buy yourself a ring. (It can be as cheap as you want: a £1 ring works as well as a £1,000 ring.) Each night before you go to bed, place the ring on your marriage finger. Feel what it is like to be married, then let yourself drift off to sleep. Choose an energy word if you wish to bring back this same feeling at any time during the day.

Creating weight loss

Creating weight loss can need sustained motivation over several months.

 1 Place your order as usual. Get a final picture of what you will look like after the weight loss. Make sure you really feel what it will be like to be slim. Check that you are moving towards what you want and not away from it. Check that your beliefs support this change. Why is it important to you to be slim?

 2 Now choose an energy word to symbolise your new slimness. For example, Slim, Attractive, Beautiful.

 3 In your mind's eye, pour positive feelings into this word. As you see it, experience the feeling again of being slim and happy.

 4 If you like, you can choose a symbol to accompany this word.

 5 Each time you bring to mind the symbol and energy word, your unconscious will remember the positive feelings of being slim and happy.

Jon's story:
The case of the winning touchdown

I was brought up in Beaver County, Pennsylvania. When I was young I used to practise throwing football with my older brother, who also played and would go on to be a star quarterback for the local high school we attended. We both loved American football, as it was normal for young boys in the community to want to grow up to be the star football player. Years before we started to practise, while I was in grade school, I always dreamt of throwing a touchdown pass to win a big game in high school. At night I would lie in bed and envision myself, under a lot of pressure and fanfare, throwing a winning score. I could feel the excitement and adrenalin rush as the crowd cheered. It was not something I consciously wanted to do – these visions appeared to be something I had already done – but I had the feeling it was to happen in the future.

About five years later, I became the first-team quarterback for my high school team, though I was not expected to play because of my small size. I never understood this, since I had always known I would be playing that role. In the biggest game of the year, the final game of the season, we were losing with time quickly

FAQs

Why is my cosmic order taking so long to manifest?

Check – have you followed all the seven steps correctly? The most common block is a belief block or a feeling block. The more emotion and positive belief you pour into your order, the stronger your intention to manifest it will be.

Have patience, your cosmic order will be delivered, or the universe may offer you something even better.

Can I stop an order I no longer want?

Yes, absolutely. The moment you stop wanting it, the universe will automatically stop its delivery. You don't have to do anything because the universe picks up your thoughts.

You can also replace and update orders. Suppose you have made a series of orders over a 12-month period. Once you receive the first order after a few months, you realise that you don't want the other orders any more, but you have a fresh vision of what you would like instead.

Simply write out your new orders following the guidelines in Step 3, and place your orders as you did before. The universe will start straight away on the delivery of your new orders.

running out and had one last down [try] against the best team in the state. We were the underdogs. The old vision then became reality, as I threw the game-winning touchdown in a game we needed to win in order to make it to the play-offs. We then went on to win the state championship. During the championship game, my first pass was a long touchdown – the excitement surrounding that day was immense as not only did we win convincingly, it was against the very same team we had beaten when I threw the first last-minute score several weeks earlier. In both games, we were counted as the underdog. I had always dreamt of playing the key role on the football field, that of quarterback. It was something I had always envisioned having happened in the past, although in reality it happened in the future.

Finally: recognise your achievements

What is the best way of knowing when you have got what you have asked for? If you have asked for something like a new car it is probably easy to spot. But maybe by the time you get it, you have forgotten exactly what you asked for.

The monkey trainer
Once upon a time there was a monkey trainer who owned two monkeys. Each day he fed them bananas. But the price of bananas was rising so he decided to cut back on food. He told his monkeys, 'Today and from now on I will only feed

*you two bananas each for breakfast, one banana for lunch
and three for dinner.'*

*The monkeys were not happy. They took their food
bowls and threw them angrily around the house. The
monkey trainer quickly tried to calm them down. 'Okay,'
he said. 'Forget it. I will feed you one banana for breakfast,
three for lunch and two for dinner.'*

*The monkeys were very happy. They picked up their
bowls and sat happily back in their cages.*

ADAPTED FROM THE CHINESE CLASSIC *THE ZHUANGZI*

Have things really changed?

Many people are so unattached to the delivery of their order
that they don't actually notice when it has been delivered. That
may seem strange, but if you place an order for a long time
ahead and then move on in your own thinking and self-development, you may discount or dismiss what happens. This is
why, when you place your order, it is very important to write
down the final piece of evidence – the one thing that will let you
know when you get your order.

The way to maintain motivation over months, years or
even decades is to consistently check where you are at each
stage of your orders, reward yourself and move on to the next
stage. You may need to sustain your belief in your orders over
a long period. Certainly, if you wish, you can always place
small, disposable, quick-delivery orders – something new for
the home perhaps.

But what if you want to be the next Gandhi or Nelson
Mandela? Sometimes what is really worth achieving may take

years. Patience is a skill that you can develop by building your own self-belief. By doing this, you can build your wisdom at the same time.

Each time an order is delivered, it is important to give yourself a pat on the back, congratulate or reward yourself for a successful order and take a look back at how far you have come. This lets the universe know that you like what you have been given and are open to more of the same. Rewarding yourself and recognising your achievement is an express way of sending a thought to the universe saying, '*Keep on going – I want more good feelings!*'

By keeping an order delivery diary, you can build up your belief that your orders will always be delivered. This is your evidence of what works for you. It will become a powerful tool to help you believe *before* you see what happens in the future, because you will have in front of you in black and white a long list of times in the past when what you asked for was delivered. This evidence will enable you to refine your orders and know when to be more specific, which orders bring you the positive feelings that you want, what you will change in future, and what you will keep.

It takes a while to build our trust in anything new – a new relationship, a new habit, a new job. Take your time and build your trust in your relationship with the cosmic ordering process. A good life-long relationship is always worth the investment of your energy.

FAQ

Can I accidentally cancel an order?

Yes. If you hold thoughts that are in conflict with your intention – your cosmic order – your focus will be on what you don't want and you will accidentally cancel your order. Remember, energy flows where your attention and focus is. If 90 per cent of your focus is on what you don't want and only 10 per cent on what you do want, the universe can't manifest the order with just 10 per cent focus.

'Remain true to your goals and allow life to carry you. That which is valuable is sometimes created slowly.'

The I Ching

✏️ Your order delivery diary

Make as many copies of this page as you like – the more the better. Write as much detail in each as possible.

Date of order

_____

What I asked for

_____

_____

_____

_____

_____

_____

Order delivery: What was delivered

_____

_____

_____

_____

_____

Date of delivery

_____

Summary Step 7

- Let go of attachment to how your order is being delivered. Keep the oven door shut. Allow yourself to accept whatever the cosmos gives you as the path to your order, including help from people, however unlikely as helpers, along the way.

- Act 'as if'. Take actions that are consistent with the assumption that your order is already in the process of being realised. Keep going in the direction of your order. From time to time you may notice synchronicities that show you that you are on track. If you are given an opportunity out of the blue and your instinct tells you to take it, make sure you do.

- Use symbols and energy words to sustain your focus.

- Keep an order delivery diary – reward yourself when an order is delivered successfully. Build your trust.

The magic formula: getting the life you want

'Our life is as our thoughts make it.'

Marcus Aurelius

By now you will have seen that the successful cosmic order is just like a delicious recipe – there are lots of different ingredients you need to include to make the perfect dish. If you miss out some, the dish may still turn out almost the same. Without others it won't work at all. But if you follow the recipe step by step, you will create just what you intended to create from the outset.

The magic formula ingredients
- **Understanding** – of the Law of Attraction and the magic of thought
- **Imagination** – to visualise your dreams
- **Desire** – to achieve them
- **Belief** – that they will come true
- **Attention and focus** – on what you want
- **Commitment** – to following the path to the end
- **Letting go and lack of attachment** – to how the outcome happens

The recipe

Step 1: Understand how the universe operates. This underlies your ability to create what you want in your life
- Remember, as you start thinking about your cosmic orders, that the universe operates according to principles and rules, including the Law of Attraction. The universe is abundant and can always provide you with what you want. You are co-creator of your own

reality and future. You create through your thoughts and the feeling you put into these.

Step 2: Decide what you want

- Identify your dreams. Use your imagination to decide what you really want, no matter what you think other people might want for you. Discover your true self. Create a picture of yourself dwelling in the midst of your goals.
- Remember the first rule of cosmic ordering: you will get what you ask for, so take care to ask for what you really want.
- Be yourself – dare to risk.

Step 3: Turn your wants into specific orders

- A wish will remain a wish until you commit to it and turn it into an order that you expect to have delivered.
- In order to make a wish into a cosmic order there are some rules to follow. Be *specific* and *detailed* about what you want to order. The more specific you are about what you want, the easier it will be for the cosmic storehouse to fulfil your order.
- Remember to write your order down using *personal* and *positively phrased* language. If you can only think of what you don't want, ask yourself, '*What do I want instead of this*?
- Check that you know *why* you want each order you write down.
- If you wish, put a date on your order. *When* do you want this?

Step 4: Take charge of your thoughts

- Add *belief* to each order. Check that your thoughts and beliefs support this intention.

- Remember the Law of Attraction – your thoughts will attract events of the same vibration. Are all your thoughts about this order positive?

- Do you really believe it is possible (not necessarily probable) for this order to come to you? Remember that the more belief you have in your order, the more focus, energy and attention will go towards it.

- Check that your order is good for you, any other people who will be affected by it, and the world at large. Set an intention that the order comes to you in a form that is to the highest good of you and all concerned.

Step 5: Access your inner power

- Go inside yourself. Practise accessing a trance or alpha state regularly. Use this state to check your level of feeling and desire about your cosmic orders. What is it you really want to experience through these? Use of the trance state will increase your attunement with the cosmos and your unconscious mind.

- Use visualisation practice to increase your general ability to visualise specific and detailed happy experiences in your life. The more you visualise regularly, the better you will be able to see the final picture of your cosmic orders when you place them.

Step 6: Place your order

- Now you are ready to place your order. Look at the cosmic order you have written down – this is what you intend to create in your life now.

- To make it manifest, start with the end in mind. Create a future memory by imagining your final picture of what you want to be given by the universe. Do this from an alpha state to increase your visualisation power.

- Write down the evidence – the one thing that will have to happen to let you know when your order has been realised? What would have to happen for you to be convinced that the order had been correctly delivered?

- Now, before you place your order, use rhythmic breathing to energise yourself so that you go to an alpha or trance state. Build your breath up so that your whole body is filled with a new energy. (See page 145 for the breathing method.)

- Next, step into (associate) the final picture of your cosmic order and experience what is going on as if it is happening to you right now. See what you see, hear what you hear, feel what you feel. Make sure that there is a positive feeling attached to the final picture.

- Now, dissociate from your order and see it as if it is a film. (See *Changing your cosmic order into a future memory*, pages 155–7)

- Place your order using the ritual of your choosing. Knowing that it is now in your future is enough. You can ask the universe to deliver your order on a specific date or at the most appropriate time of the cosmos's choosing. (See *Six ways to press the 'send' button*, pages 159-62.)

- Continue to breathe from your whole body into your intention.
- Thank the universe for already realising your order. See it already present in your future as a memory about to be realised.

Step 7: Let the universe decide the how

- Let go of attachment *as soon as* you have placed your order. Know that everything is unfolding as it should. You don't have to keep checking that your order is in process. It is enough to place your order once.
- You have decided the *what*. The universe decides the *how*.
- It is okay to take actions. In fact it is important to take actions consistent with the belief that your order will be delivered.
- Make sure that you '*act as if*' – act in the expectation that your dream will come true. Allow yourself to accept whatever the cosmos gives you as the path to your order, including help from people, however unlikely as helpers, along the way.
- Use symbols and energy words to sustain your focus while you are waiting for your order to be delivered.
- Keep an order delivery diary – reward yourself when an order is delivered successfully. Build your trust in your own ability to manifest.
- Have patience – some orders will manifest in days, others may take decades.

Making your life better

Now you fully understand the process of cosmic ordering, you can use the magic formula in your life daily, weekly, monthly and for the rest of your life.

If you would like to rewrite any of your orders in the light of all you have learnt, below are some new life lists for you to use.

My updated life lists: my cosmic orders

Relationships

What do I want? My cosmic orders.

_____

_____

_____

_____

_____

_____

When do I want it?

_____

_____

My final picture/piece of evidence that will let me know I have it.

_____

_____

_____

_____

Career

What do I want? My cosmic orders.

_____

_____

_____

When do I want it?

_____

_____

My final picture/piece of evidence that will let me know I have it.

_____

_____

_____

_____

Money

What do I want? My cosmic orders.

When do I want it?

My final picture/piece of evidence that will let me know I have it.

Health and fitness

What do I want? My cosmic orders.

When do I want it?

My final picture/piece of evidence that will let me know I
have it.

Spiritual and personal development

What do I want? My cosmic orders.

_____

_____

_____

_____

_____

When do I want it?

_____

_____

My final picture/piece of evidence that will let me know I
have it.

_____

_____

_____

_____

_____

_____

_____

Choose any area of your life

What do I want? My cosmic orders.

When do I want it?

My final picture/piece of evidence that will let me know I
have it.

Clearing a permanent path to your dreams

'People are always blaming their circumstances for what they are. I don't believe in circumstances. The people who get on in this world are the people who get up and look for the circumstances they want, and if they can't find them, they make them.'

GEORGE BERNARD SHAW

Using cosmic ordering

Once you start to use cosmic ordering and see what it can bring you in your life, you can extend its use to many different situations. You can use it to find solutions for problems, to find communication within difficult relationships, to bring you new possessions, and to realise your dreams. The limits are only within your imagination.

Before long, you will discover that your life starts to gain a new energy and vigour. With each order you place – if you really pay attention to ordering wisely – the amount of positive feeling in your life will increase and the amount of negative feeling will decrease. Your life can take off in a way that you could never have imagined.

An analogy for this is to think of the momentum that builds when you make a snowball. Imagine that you are standing in a snow-covered landscape. Far below you is a valley and you are standing at the top of the hill.

The path up to the top of the hill was rocky at times, but you reached the top because you wanted to go down to the valley, which you believed would be beautiful. Here you are, finally able to look at the valley and there it is – at the bottom of the valley a beautiful lush meadow awaits you, full of the promise of a wonderful life.

Now, you must find the way down from the hill to the bottom of the valley or turn back and forget about your dream. It is a long way down. It looks as rocky as the path you just came up. You can turn back, or continue. What do you do?

Then you suddenly realise that it doesn't matter that there are rocks. To clear this path, you already have all the resources you need because you can use the snow right there around you.

You bend down and pick up a handful of snow and make a tiny snowball. Then you take another handful and make the snowball bigger. You add handful after handful of snow and roll it along the ground so it becomes larger and larger. When it is big enough, you intentionally let it go with determination and focus down the side of the hill. As the snowball rolls down the hillside, it gathers more snow around itself and increases in speed, rolling faster and faster. About halfway down the hill, it is so big and so fast that it becomes an avalanche that is so strong that all the rocks and boulders that blocked the way down are simply swept up in its advance.

The path is now clear, and you can walk down through to the valley and its delights – the valley you always wanted to see.

This chapter covers a few final thoughts on other ways you can use cosmic ordering in your life. When you use any of the following exercises, you are likely to see results very quickly – within hours or days.

And because you are an amazing person, with an avalanche of resources, you will probably come up with your own thoughts on how to use cosmic ordering in your life.

Problem-solving using cosmic ordering

Problem-solving is made easy with cosmic ordering. As with any cosmic order, the key is to focus on what you want, rather than what you don't want. Your final picture in the case of a problem will be the solution you want – and ultimately the solution your unconscious believes is possible.

 Sit down and relax. Spend some time breathing or relaxing your body until you can feel that you have entered a mild meditative or trance state. You will know when you reach this state, because you will begin to be much more focused on the internal pictures inside your head, and your attention will move away from external distractions and sounds and towards your own inner thoughts. State to the cosmos that your intention is to find a solution for whatever is bothering you today and that the solution will be delivered by the cosmos within whatever time frame you specify.

 Firstly, review all the details you have in your mind about the problem. Visualise yourself in the problem situation, doing, having or being the problem. But, in order that you keep some distance from the problem, dissociate, that is imagine that you can see yourself in this situation as if you are in the audience of a play, sitting in the back row and the problem is being performed on a stage at some distance in front of you. You can see everything happening, but obviously the main players look quite small.

 Now imagine that the lights are turned off and the main characters leave the stage. You might even want to see the stagehands taking the scenery away so that the stage is totally empty.

 Change your seat in the theatre. This time you may want to move a bit closer so you can see what is going to happen in the next act more clearly. This is going to be a much happier drama altogether. Perhaps you want to change your perspective as well. If you are sitting in the centre of a row of seats, why not change to the side. If you are on the right, change to the left.

If you are on the left side, change to the right. In fact, why not take a seat in the front row. You deserve the most expensive seat in the house, don't you?

 5 Now see the stage being filled with action once more. There you are in the middle of the stage. But this time, the problem has already been solved. It's a happy, joyful scene. Good things are happening to you, the main character. The stage lights may start dimly or the stage may be fully lit straight away. The old problem has completely disappeared from your view to be replaced entirely by this new solution. Trust your unconscious to connect with the cosmos and to deliver this solution to you.

 6 You can at this point imagine the solution with a date attached, or you can ask the cosmos to deliver the solution at the earliest date and in a way that is to your highest good.

 7 Spend some minutes sitting imagining the solution fully present in your life and playing out in front of you. Check with your instinct to see whether you can add anything to the picture that will bring you even more positive feelings. You may want to add the intention that the solution is delivered in this way, or any even better way that the cosmos can find to deliver it.

8 Finally, remember to thank the universe in advance for the delivery of this order.

Resolving conflict

When you are having a conflict or miscommunication with someone, the following technique can be used to ask the cosmos to deliver an order in the form of improved understanding, communication, or a generally improved relationship.

1 Sit down and relax. Once again, spend some time practising rhythmic breathing, or relaxing your body until you can feel that you have entered an alpha or trance state. At the point you enter the trance, you will feel that your conscious mind has slowed and you will be able to focus fully on one idea.

2 Ask your unconscious to bring to mind the situation with the person you are having difficulty with. Imagine that they are standing in front of you as you review the current situation.

3 Clear the screen and ask the universe for whatever you want – increased understanding, new communication, or simply a happy resolution of the conflict between the two of you.

4 Now visualise a new scene – what you want instead. See the two of you standing side by side. There is now a cord between your heart and the heart of the other person. Let your unconscious mind provide you with the positive words and feelings that will replace the old situation. Notice what you see, hear and feel.

What are you now saying to the person that has resolved the old situation? What is he/she saying to you that has resolved the old situation?

5 Trust that whatever you see, the universe can deliver.

6 Thank the universe in advance for the delivery of this cosmic order.

7 Expect the unexpected. You may hear from the person

by telephone, or simply find that the next time they speak to you it feels entirely different.

Resolving anxiety

This third technique can be used to resolve anxiety. You can also adapt the technique for any situation where you are feeling a negative emotion and wish to raise your general level of positive feelings.

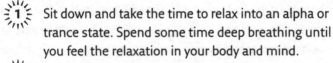

1 Sit down and take the time to relax into an alpha or trance state. Spend some time deep breathing until you feel the relaxation in your body and mind.

2 Now, briefly (for a few seconds only) bring to mind a film of the situation that you were feeling anxious about. As you watch this film, make sure you can see your body in the picture as if it is a story, so that you are dissociated.

3 Now clear the screen in your mind's eye, knowing as you do this that this is the last time you ever have to think of the situation in that way.

4 Now, in full communication with your unconscious mind, think of a new, happy situation after the anxiety has been resolved. It could be an hour after the anxiety is resolved, a day, or a week. Trust your unconscious to come up with the right answer for you.

5 Associate into the picture – that is, as you experience the situation, feel what you feel, see what you see, hear what you hear as if you are looking through your own eyes. From this vantage point, you can if you want to look back at the old situation where you felt anxious and see what it was you did that resolved it.

Or you can simply luxuriate in the new situation, feeling all the positive feelings you are feeling, knowing that these positive feelings will continue to be present in your life from now into the future.

 Thank the universe in advance for delivering your cosmic order.

Making a decision

You can use a similar process to the previous technique if you are stuck on a decision and want to ask your unconscious to put in an order that will give you the best result.

 Relax and go to your alpha state (a good time to do this is before you go to bed at night). Take all the time you need.

 Bring to mind the issue and the two options. Imagine that you can see them as two paths going in different directions towards different futures.

 Now, imagine taking the first path. Where does it lead? How does it feel?

 Next, take the second path. Where does it lead? How does it feel?

 Ask your unconscious if there is a third path you can take. Note the answer.

 Now clear the picture. Bring up a picture of an empty screen in front of you.

 Ask your unconscious to tune into the universe and bring up whatever solution and decision is to your highest good right now. You may see a picture or have a feeling.

8 Ask the universe to remove all other options from your life.

 9 Thank the universe in advance that the decision will be made for you within three days.

 10 Notice what events happen. Be aware of synchronicities. Take any opportunities that feel right to your gut instinct.

 11 If a result does not come fully as you would like it within around three days, repeat the process.

Use these techniques regularly at the same time as making orders from your Life Lists and you will soon notice a huge improvement in the positive feelings you have about your life.

Mapping the future for the rest of your life

Why not place orders for the rest of your life? The further ahead you place an order the less attached you will be to it. Most people place orders too soon and make them too small. Thinking far ahead will allow you to really stretch your thinking so that you can truly create the destiny you want without censoring your dreams in any way.

 1 Before beginning this exercise, relax. You may want to meditate or breathe for a while to increase your connection with the cosmos. Remember, the more you can get in touch with your inner knowing and the feeling of what you want, the more effective it will be.

☀ **2** In your mind's eye see your future stretching in front of you like a timeline. Imagine that you can rise above your future and fly over each decade so that you can look down and notice what memories are already in your future. How does your future feel right now? How many decades ahead can you see?

☀ **3** If you can't see as far ahead as you want to, simply imagine stretching out your time line so that it grows and extends further. How far do you want to go? 90 years old? 100 years old? 110? 120?

☀ **4** Come back to now. Bring back all your future memories.

☀ **5** Now, just imagine that you can have anything you want over the rest of your life. What would make each decade perfect? What do you want to feel more of? To have more of? To be more of? To do more of?

☀ **6** Write down any immediate thoughts that come to mind.

☀ **7** Now, in the worksheet below divide your ideas into the different areas of your life they relate to. What could you ask for in your life that would enable you to give each area a big ten out of ten in terms of your satisfaction?

☀ **8** Now set your intentions for the rest of your life. For each one, check:

- Do you have a picture of what you want? What does what you want feel like? Look like? Smell like? Taste like? Sound like?
- How will you know when you have accepted delivery of your cosmic order? What is the one

piece of evidence in your final order that when it happens will remind you that you have just accepted delivery?

- Write each of your wants down on the worksheet below. Describe each picture in as much detail as possible. Make sure that you can really feel what it is like when you have it.

- Remember not to limit yourself in any way. If the worksheet isn't big enough, make your own. You can have as many orders as you want, or as few.

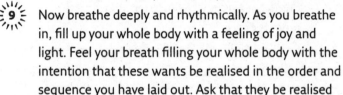 **9** Now breathe deeply and rhythmically. As you breathe in, fill up your whole body with a feeling of joy and light. Feel your breath filling your whole body with the intention that these wants be realised in the order and sequence you have laid out. Ask that they be realised in a way that is in accordance with the highest good of all concerned.

10 Send your orders in whatever way you prefer (see *Pressing send* pages 159–62). You can send each one in turn or post them together.

11 Send yourself your own order acknowledgement. Thank the universe for the fact that it has accepted, and is already in the process of delivering, your orders. Let go of all attachment.

12 Why not place an order for each decade or year of your future and make every moment of your future memorable?

Area of life

Date   **Age**

What do I want?

My final picture (What does it feel like? Look like? Smell like? Taste like? Sound like?) including the one thing/piece of evidence that will let me know that my order has been delivered

'*Every king springs from a race of slaves, and every slave has had kings among his ancestors.*'

PLATO